Thank Everybody
for Everything!

☙

Grow Your Life and Business
with Gratitude

DEBORAH E. ROSER AND

PEGGY R. HOYT

*Kathy,
Thank you!
Peggy & Debbie*

Thank Everybody for Everything!
Grow Your Life and Business with Gratitude

ISBN 978-0-9823220-0-0

Copyright © 2009 by Deborah E. Roser and Peggy R. Hoyt

Published by Gratitude Partners, LLC
2655 Curryville Road
Chuluota, Florida 32766
Phone (407) 977-8080
Fax (407) 977-8078

For more information or to order a copy of this book,
visit *ThankEverybodyForEverything.com*
or call 407.977.8080

Printed in the United States of America.
All rights reserved under International Copyright Law. Contents and/or cover may not be reproduced in whole or in part, in any form or by any means without the express written consent of the Publisher.

Book Design by Julie Hoyt Dorman
www.dormangraphics.com

Dedication

This book is dedicated to everyone
who lifts, encourages and inspires others
with the gift of gratitude.

Our Appreciation

We send our appreciation to Radeen Cochran for her time, expert editing skills and valuable suggestions. She selflessly dedicated countless hours to help us improve every aspect of this endeavor and for that we are grateful. Thank you, Radeen!

Like Debbie and her husband Craig, Radeen and her husband, Hayden, are sailors. The Rosers and the Cochrans met as a result of their mutual love of sailing Island Packet sailboats. Radeen is an elementary school librarian and Hayden is a high school teacher. They enjoy spending their summers cruising in the waters of the Chesapeake Bay and New England aboard their Island Packet, *Island Spirit*.

TABLE OF CONTENTS

Dedication iii

Appreciation iv

Introduction vii

Chapter 1 – Appreciation and Gratitude 1
EXERCISE ONE: *Reflect on your life and a time when you felt appreciation for something or someone.*

Chapter 2 – Is Gratitude Important? 7
EXERCISE TWO: *Think of family or friends who seem genuinely and consistently happy.*

Chapter 3 – Why Do Some Refuse to Express Gratitude? 15
EXERCISE THREE: *Think of a recent time when someone appreciated you.*

Chapter 4 – Gratitude and the Law of Attraction 23

Chapter 5 – Finding the Gratitude Within 35
EXERCISE FOUR: *Reflect about family, friends, home and activities you are grateful for.*

EXERCISE FIVE: *Start noticing the blessings around you, from the moment you get out of bed in the morning.*

EXERCISE SIX: *Start thanking everybody for everything.*

Chapter 6 – Making Gratitude Your Attitude 49
EXERCISE SEVEN: *Identify three things to be grateful for every day and share them with someone and ask that person share theirs with you.*

EXERCISE EIGHT: *Start a gratitude journal.*

Chapter 7 – Expressing Gratitude **57**
EXERCISE NINE: Write a letter of gratitude and deliver it in person!

Chapter 8 – Making a Living through Giving **75**
EXERCISE TEN: List everything you do to show appreciation to your current and potential clients or customers and referral sources.

Chapter 9 – Appreciation Marketing
and Relationship Marketing **95**
EXERCISE ELEVEN: Today thank a client/customer/referral source for their business. Do the same tomorrow and every day following.

EXERCISE TWELVE: Today thank someone at work for something you feel is simply part of their job. Do the same thing tomorrow and every day following.

EXERCISE THIRTEEN: At your company meetings, begin with a positive round—what's going well—and end with recognition and appreciation.

Chapter 10 – Thank Everybody for Everything! **101**

Appendix A – Gratitude Exercises (compiled) **107**

Appendix B – Resources and Recommended Reading ... **111**

About the Authors **113**

Gratitude Expressions — Your Five-year
Gratitude Journal **117**

INTRODUCTION

> A person starts to live
> when he lives outside himself.
>
> — ALBERT SCHWEITZER

Welcome to *Thank Everybody for Everything! Grow Your Life and Business with Gratitude*. We appreciate your interest in gratitude and the importance it can have in your life.

When we decided to write this book, we knew it would be important to start with a discussion about the value of gratitude as a part of daily life in general. We will consider the meaning of gratitude, the advantages of experiencing genuine appreciation and the expression of gratitude for your circumstances and for the people in your life. We also know "there is nothing new under the sun." Psychologists and others have been studying the benefits of gratitude for decades. There are many wonderful books on the subject. We want to happily jump on the bandwagon that is teaching and promoting the value of experiencing genuine appreciation and expressing gratitude, even as we all struggle to get through a challenging and historic economic time.

For many in today's economy, life has become so difficult it is impossible to recognize anything worth appreciating. Here, too, we also find nothing new under the sun. As long as humans have inhabited the earth, people have suffered loss and pain. Even in what we consider good economic times, there are those who suffer, whether from emotional or physical pain, oppression or poverty or some other adversity. What we find extraordinary is when we hear about people who experience tremendous loss, and yet their outlook on life remains positive and allows them to enjoy a happiness and success unrivaled by some who have not suffered near the same degree of anguish and pain. Why is this? Is it because, "You don't know what you've got 'til it's gone?" or for other reasons? For some, life certainly does go unappreciated until it's almost out of reach. For others, appreciation is as natural and life-sustaining as the air they breathe, and they will let no person and no circumstance rob them of that emotion.

We believe every aspect of life should be filled with appreciation and expressions of gratitude, both giving and receiving, not only because there is so much to be thankful for but also because life can and will be better for it. Quite simply, we believe in thanking everybody for everything! Nothing is so insignificant that we can't find appreciation for it. That includes gratitude and appreciation in our personal lives as well as in our business lives, whether we are talking about family and friends or employees, bosses, colleagues and clients or customers. You will enjoy improved success in life, and in business, when you add genuine appreciation and expressions of gratitude to your life principles.

A person enlightened with the attitude of gratitude will enrich the lives of others with the same attitude of gratitude. Imagine the possibilities as genuine appreciation and expressions of gratitude are paid forward. We invite you to join us on a path that will lead to more joy and success, not only in your life, but in the lives of those you touch.

We hope you will adopt the following as a mantra for your daily life—Thank everybody for everything!

༺

I asked for strength
that I might achieve;

I was made weak
that I might learn humbly to obey.

I asked for health
that I might do greater things;

I was given infirmity
that I might do better things.

I asked for riches
that I might be happy;

I was given poverty
that I might be wise.

I asked for power
that I might have the praise of men;

I was given weakness
that I might feel the need of God.

I asked for all things
that I might enjoy life;

I was given life
that I might enjoy all things.

I got nothing that I had asked for,
but everything that I had hoped for.

Almost despite myself,
my unspoken prayers were answered;

I am, among all men,
most richly blessed.

—PRAYER OF AN UNKNOWN
CONFEDERATE SOLDIER

ॐ

*Be the change
you want to see in the world.*

— GHANDI

x Thank Everybody for Everything!

CHAPTER 1

☙

Appreciation and Gratitude

*As one person
I cannot change the world,
but I can change
the world of one person.*
—PAUL SHANE SPEAR

What *are* appreciation and gratitude? We thought this would be a good place to start a book that focuses on the benefits of appreciation and gratitude. However, providing a basic definition of these two words is not rocket science. Any dictionary can provide the meaning of these words.

According to Wikipedia, "gratitude, thankfulness, or appreciation is an emotion that occurs after people receive help, depending on how they interpret the situation. Specifically, gratitude is experienced if people perceive the help they receive as (a) valuable to them, (b) costly to their benefactor, and (c) given by the benefactor with benevolent intentions (rather than ulterior motives)." We believe this is a basic and accurate definition we can all accept.

But this book is not about definitions and is not written simply to provide a roadmap to success by teaching everyone how to say "thank you." No real success can come from such simplicity or shallow principles. Success cannot emerge from empty words. Instead, this book is meant to provide a journey to find within ourselves the true feeling, purpose and value of genuine appreciation for all of the blessings in our lives. And as we look inside ourselves, so we shall see inside others.

> What lies behind us
> and what lies before us
> are tiny matters compared to
> what lies within us.
> — RALPH WALDO EMERSON

As important as it is to discuss what appreciation and gratitude are, it is equally important to discuss what they are not, especially in the context of business and especially if you want your business to be successful. Appreciation and gratitude are not simply saying "thanks" when you believe it is the right response to a given situation. They are not mere words. We do not believe you should use language to attempt to manipulate others through flattery.

Appreciation and gratitude are also not only positive thinking. Reaping the emotional and other rewards of appreciation and gratitude requires more than just going through the motions. Genuine appreciation is heartfelt—an emotion that comes from the heart, as well as the mind. It is a selfless expression that seeks no reward and, has no expectations. It arises purely and innocently from the authentic recognition of the importance of the gift given, as well as the significance of the gift giver.

Genuine appreciation cannot be learned from a book or other external source. It must come from an internal understanding, and it must be cultivated and constructed into a valued principle. For some this is easy, almost as natural as breathing. For others, expressing appreciation and gratitude seems frivolous and of no value. Life is simply too difficult, with one problem after another, to express true gratitude.

For those who may be struggling to find anything worthy of appreciation or who may simply have come to take blessings for granted, we invite you to take a walk down memory lane. Use the exercise below to allow your memory to guide you back to a time when you once experienced this valued emotion. If you find this difficult, try to find at least one moment when you felt genuine appreciation for something or someone. We can all find something to be grateful for. According to a Minquass American Indian saying, "If you see no reason for giving thanks, the fault lies in yourself."

We believe each and every one of us has felt genuine appreciation at some time for something. You may not have thought specifically about what you appreciate in a long time. You may have allowed life's circumstances to get in the way of remembering. By doing this exercise, you will be transported to a time in your life when someone did something special for you, perhaps recently, perhaps long ago. Your efforts will not go unrewarded.

EXERCISE ONE: *Find time and a quiet place where you can reflect in private, with uninterrupted peace. Reflect on your life—think of a time when you felt appreciation for something or someone. That time may be the present. That time may have been when you were in high school and had an inspiring teacher or coach. That time may have been the day your first child was born or when someone helped you in a time of need. Try to keep old or present negative emotions from blocking your memory. For this exercise, you are simply having a conversation with yourself. You don't have to share this conversation with anyone else, so be free with your thoughts and your feelings. Focus on remembering at least one instance of feeling genuine appreciation. When you find that moment, close your eyes, go back to the event and feel the emotion you felt then. Now, as that emotion consumes your heart and mind and brings you joy, you have the answer to the question—What are appreciation and gratitude?*

The need for gratitude is universal. Everyone everywhere craves recognition, validation and appreciation from others. Mother Teresa once said "There is more hunger for love and appreciation in this world than for bread." We believe that's true. Just as you need to be appreciated, so does each and every person you encounter every day, whether on the street, in your home or in your office.

This is the first step. You have experienced the emotion of genuine appreciation, and you likely now understand that everyone everywhere needs appreciation as much as you do. Armed with this powerful knowledge, we will learn later that gratitude fully expressed is transformative. It creates profound connections and affirms and strengthens our relationships with others. It is also as much a gift to yourself as it is to the intended recipient, and so has the power to create an unbroken cycle of giving and receiving joy. ෆ

༄

Everything is given to me
and I pass it on.

You must give
if you want to receive.

Let the center of your being
be one of giving, giving, giving.

You can't give too much,
and you will discover
you cannot give
without receiving.

— PEACE PILGRIM

CHAPTER 2

ଔ

Is Gratitude Important?

> You have it easily in your power
> To increase the sum total of
> this world's happiness now.
> How? By giving a few words
> of appreciation to someone
> who is lonely or discouraged.
> Perhaps you will forget tomorrow
> the kind words you say today,
> But the recipient may cherish them
> over a lifetime.
>
> — DALE CARNEGIE

Is gratitude important? It seems like a simple question and if you did the exercise in Chapter One, we would expect a resounding, "Yes!" However, one exercise won't fully make our point. In fact, some of you may be thinking, "Bah humbug!" The reality is that most people do not practice the expression of gratitude every day. In preparing to write this book, we asked people randomly what they were grateful for and far too many had to think long and hard!

We tend to take for granted the little things in life, like a bright sunny day, a smile from a stranger or the kindness of a door held open. And in our harried lives, too often we overlook the big things as well. It hardly makes sense to overlook the obvious, but we do. We will explore some of the reasons why later. For now you may wonder, if you've gone this long without noticing, and expressing appreciation for the blessings in your life and you've managed to survive, does this appreciation thing really add any real value? For that matter, if you can't even keep your head above water in these tough economic times and you use every spare moment just thinking and worrying about your financial condition, what good is looking for blessings, if any even exist? Isn't the truth simply that some people are just luckier than others? That would be the easy answer, wouldn't it?

It may seem that life is easier if we just accept our fate and not expend effort to look for and count our blessings. We're never going to be "lucky" and isn't it always easier to do "nothing?" You may be surprised to learn there is no such thing as doing "nothing." Choosing not to make a choice is making a choice. Choosing to do "nothing" is choosing to do something—choosing the default position. If you choose not to go grocery shopping, you choose to eat nothing or whatever is left in your cupboard. If you choose not to pursue a better position at work or in the job market, you choose to maintain your present position and present salary. If you are in debt and choose not to get a second job or change your spending habits, you choose to stay in debt. You may perceive these choices as easy, but the results can be disastrous. It is the same with consciously choosing gratitude and appreciation for the bounty in your life.

When it comes to personal development, choosing the default position by doing "nothing" has consequences you may not want to live with. In this case, when we fail to make the effort to see the blessings in our world, we accept and can even invite negative energy and situations into our lives *and* into the lives of those around us. Whatever your situation—good or bad—accepting your situation perpetuates your situation. When we find ourselves in less than ideal circumstances, it is easier to blame external events than to look inside and try to change our outlook. Complain, complain, complain… it's easy, but where has that ever gotten anyone?! If you are willing to make at least a small conscious effort up front, you will find the rewards of gratitude and appreciation are immeasurable and duplicative.

> In our daily lives, we must see that it is not happiness that makes us grateful, but the gratefulness that makes us happy.
> —ALBERT CLARKE

Deborah Norville pointed out in her book, *Thank You Power*, that people who participated in one gratitude study "were brighter, more optimistic, more hopeful—more positive," and "[p]eople experiencing positive affect are more confident and energetic. They feel their lives are going well, that they are meeting the goals they've set for themselves and dealing with the challenges that come along the way. They are more outgoing. They are, in a word, *happier*."

EXERCISE TWO: *Think about friends or family members who seem genuinely and consistently happy. Think especially of happy people who are not necessarily wealthy. Think of happy people who have suffered loss or serious illness. Do you find them generally to be people who exhibit positive or negative tendencies? Is their glass half full or half empty? Are their conversations centered around complaining or do they seem to be continually exploring and moving forward? Do they speak of blessings in their lives? Do they seem generally to enjoy and be grateful for people and circumstances? If you cannot find any happy people who are not wealthy and have not suffered loss, can you determine which came first... the wealth or the happiness... the wealth or the blessings? Seriously, were they born with a silver spoon? Have you never seen them cry? Go ahead and ask them if they feel blessed—and the role gratitude plays in their life. You might be surprised by the answer!*

So can you identify any benefits of expressing gratitude? Remember how you felt in your heart and mind when, in doing Exercise One, you recalled and re-experienced at least one instance of feeling appreciation for someone or something? Was that a bad feeling? Did you conjure up images of dragons and monsters? Or were you instead relaxed and joyful? Did you wish you never had that experience? Or did you want more?

Are we happier when we give appreciation—when we feel thankful to and about another person? You bet! Why? Because when we feel appreciation, that means we have noticed something good. When we notice the good, there's less room in our mind and in our heart for the bad. When we notice the good, we have less time for the bad. The glass begins to fill. Indeed, gratitude insulates you from the negativity.

> *Both abundance and lack
> exist simultaneously in our lives,
> as parallel realities.
> It is always our conscious choice
> which secret garden we will tend...
> when we choose not to focus
> on what is missing from our lives
> but are grateful for the
> abundance that's present—
> love, health, family, friends, work,
> the joys of nature and personal pursuits
> that bring us pleasure—
> the wasteland of illusion falls away
> and we experience Heaven on earth.*
>
> — SARAH BAN BREATHNACH

What would it be like to go through life experiencing joyful moment after joyful moment just because you were capable of noticing and appreciating the blessings in your life—everything from the freshness after a spring shower to the vibrant colors of autumn to watching your daughter take her first steps to still having a job in one of the worst economic times our nation has ever experienced? Is having joy in your life important? If your answer is yes, would you then consider that the blessings in your life, and your recognition and appreciation of those blessings are important? If you think so, then we have our resounding yes—gratitude *is* important! Now, imagine duplicating your joy once a month... or once a week... or even, once a day!

> ଓଃ
> *The more you recognize
> and express gratitude
> for the things you have,
> the more you will have
> to express gratitude for.*
> — ZIG ZIGLAR

To appreciate and to be appreciated are equally important and equally joyful. As important as it is to notice and appreciate the blessings in our lives, it is also personally very rewarding to be appreciated. When we do a good deed or a kindness that is noticed and appreciated, we feel valued and validated. Our worth is affirmed. It is important to us that we bring happiness to the lives of others and it is important that we mean something to others as well.

So whether we are receiving or giving appreciation, the result is a feeling of good or a good feeling. We have never met a person who felt bad or blue because he was appreciated or expressed appreciation for a blessing or a gift from another, have you? Feeling good has its own rewards.

> ଓଃ
> *When the heart is full of gratitude,
> there is little room
> left for despair.*
> — ST. PAUL

In another study Deborah Norville wrote about in *Thank You Power*, Dr. Alice Isen, the nation's leading researcher on positive affect, looked at the side effects when people feel good. Among other things, Dr. Isen found that positive emotions make people more helpful to others. And since helping someone else makes people feel good about what they have done, the positive feelings continue and even amplify, creating more good feelings. Remember the cycle of giving and receiving joy we talked about earlier?

So why is gratitude important? First, it satisfies a craving in all of us to be recognized and considered important. Second, it brings us joy, whether we are the recipient of appreciation or we are expressing appreciation. If you have our *Gratitude Expressions* journal, you will see one quote on each of its 366 pages, one for each day of the year, including Leap Year. Although they are too numerous to include in this book, each and every one of those quotes is a testament to the overwhelming recognition of the positive benefits of gratitude and the absolute uselessness of ingratitude. Gratitude may very well be so important that a life without it is a life destined for gloom and misery. ᘓ

ᘓ

*If it is a new thought to you
that gratitude brings your whole mind
into closer harmony
with the creative energies
of the universe,
consider it well,
and you will see that it is true.*
— WALLACE WATTLES

CHAPTER 3

❦

Why Do Some Refuse to Express Gratitude?

*When a person
doesn't have gratitude
something is missing
in his or her humanity.
A person can almost be defined by
his or her attitude of gratitude.*

—ELIE WIESEL, HOLOCAUST SURVIVOR

There are many reasons why people shy away from feeling or showing appreciation or gratitude. If you have difficulty finding the blessings in your life or have difficulty expressing gratitude, perhaps you already know what the obstacles are that prevent you from experiencing these attributes. We don't pretend to know how to counsel anyone on overcoming all of the obstacles in their lives. We are, however, big proponents of taking affirmative steps to deal with obstacles and challenges so life is always on a course toward improvement.

The first step toward overcoming any challenge is to recognize its existence. If we cannot see it, we cannot get beyond it. If we do not know it exists, we cannot address it. Though we are not psychologists or counselors, we *are* going to question and challenge your belief system. Let's start with an exercise to remind us how it feels to be appreciated.

EXERCISE THREE: *Identify at least one instance—more if you can—when someone in the past few days genuinely recognized you with appreciation or gratitude. Look back farther if you need to. Did anyone—a relative, a clerk in a store—say thank you to you today? Did someone recognize a project you completed—whether a report at work or a well-cooked meal at home? Did a neighbor tell you how nice your garden looks? Did someone wave to you while sitting in traffic when you allowed him or her in? Did you get an award or promotion recently? Did the postman, a neighbor or even a total stranger smile and wave at you for seemingly no reason at all? How does it feel to be recognized or appreciated?*

As we continue to talk about why it may be difficult for some to notice or appreciate blessings, try to remember how it felt for you to be appreciated. Later, we will provide some exercises and ideas that might help with overcoming at least some of life's obstacles by helping to cultivate genuine appreciation.

An obstacle is something that impedes progress or improvement. Make no mistake—everyone has obstacles or challenges. Often, we have the same obstacles and challenges. While a student at the University of Central Florida, Debbie served on the Orientation Team. That summer she learned a life lesson about obstacles. This is how she describes it:

> It was our job to orient the incoming freshman students to the university. We had to acquaint them with the physical environment of the university as well as the emotional

environment of university life. Our trainer, Jimmy Ferrell, was one of the best and most caring personal development trainers most of us would ever meet. After a summer of extraordinary personal development training as well as learning everything we could about the university, it was time to start the orientation program with the incoming freshmen. Our program was to take place over two days. For the first exercise, we broke into groups, with each team leader taking 6 or 7 freshmen into a circle. We were in the auditorium and there were about 35 groups. Each group had to come up with a list of concerns they had about entry into college life. These were the potential "obstacles" to their success at college.

I recall my group came up with several—the students were concerned they would not be able to manage their time, would not know anyone, would not fit in and would not be smart enough, to name a few. After sufficient time had passed for everyone to complete their list, Jimmy stood in front of the auditorium and, going from one group to another, asked each for one concern from their list. After the first few groups recited concerns, we started hearing the same concerns over and over. This was an "aha" moment for many of the freshmen. It was obvious that not only did everyone there have obstacles but that everyone pretty much had the *same* obstacles. This was a tremendously important first lesson for them. The freshmen quickly learned they were not as alone as they originally thought. You could almost hear a collective sigh of relief!

Like incoming freshmen to college, we all have obstacles. And many of us have the same obstacles, no matter the issue. We are not nearly as alone as we think we are. So let's start with the acceptance and understanding of ourselves as we take a look at some of the obstacles to recognizing and appreciating blessings.

First, look at the relationship between vendors or service providers (we will call them all vendors) and their customers or clients (we will call them all customers). Let's assume that the vendors provide a good product at a fair price and with good service. We will also assume the customer is not difficult or offensive. In this relationship, some customers may believe they owe no special gratitude to the vendor, because they pay for the product they receive. If one vendor offers a better price or better service, well, that's just good old fashioned competition not deserving of any particular recognition. The price paid is all the "appreciation" that is necessary. On the other side of that relationship, some vendors may believe they owe no special thanks to their customers, because they provide a valuable product for the price paid. If their customers do not like the way they are treated, well, they can just go elsewhere.

The dichotomy here is that most customers want to be appreciated for patronizing the vendor and most vendors would like to be appreciated for providing a valued product to the community. As we already mentioned, it is a basic human craving to be appreciated. Just because we are talking about a business relationship, we sometimes forget we are dealing with humans on both sides of the relationship. The reality is the demand for appreciation can be selfish and blind to the equally important need of the person on the other side of the relationship to be acknowledged. Imagine a customer and a vendor facing each other as if staring at a mirror, each feeling they are entitled to the other's appreciation and not recognizing the same need in the other. Do you see them scowling? Or do they appear haughty? Have you ever seen yourself in either role? Do you see someone else, maybe a vendor or a customer you have dealt with? What possible reason could there be for one to be more entitled to appreciation than the other? Frankly, there isn't any! What obstacle would cloud that perspective? Is it lack of compassion? Is the pace of life too fast? Are we afraid of appearing needy or indebted? In the final analysis, if neither is entitled to any appreciation, at best, the relationship is bland; at worst, the relationship is over. If, on the other hand, both are entitled to receive appreciation and they do, in fact, receive the appreciation they deserve, then the relationship will thrive and grow.

Along the same lines, some employers or supervisors may believe they owe no special gratitude to their employees. They pay their employees for doing a good job. Their compensation is appreciation enough. Notwithstanding that belief, money has never been the best motivator. Author Bob Nelson aptly pointed out, "People may take a job for more money, but they often leave it for more recognition." Remember, as much as you crave appreciation, so do others, regardless of position or life station, yours or theirs.

In these examples or in others you can think of, some may believe if they show appreciation, they will be beholden or indebted to that person. If they recognize the gift or nicety provided to them by another, they may have to return the same kindness, and that can cause anxiety. Some others may believe if they show appreciation, they will be perceived as weak or needy. They will appear dependent on others when they have been raised to be independent and self-sufficient. However, unless the "gift" was given with an expectation of reciprocity or with any other ulterior motive, which it never should be, the gift giver would likely be offended or saddened if your true and sole response was a feeling of indebtedness or if you were left with a feeling of inferiority.

This ties into what we believe is another profound human need—the need to be needed and the need to do good. While many of us are raised to be independent, the dichotomy is we all need to be needed. We need to feel connected. If we are needed, we have the opportunity to do good. If we do good, we are contributing to society. If we are contributing to society, we connect with the universe.

When you show genuine appreciation to another, you elevate that person's spirits and self-confidence, likely to such a degree the person who just gave you the gift may now feel connected to you and/or the universe! Genuine appreciation itself becomes a gift.

By the way, we wonder if some amount of dependency is all bad. If we all need to be needed, is it rational to go through life as though we don't need anyone? And do we really believe we could survive without the help of others? It is wise and good to be smart and strong and capable of handling your life and your affairs, but not so independent that you don't need anybody for anything. If that were true, where would you get your job, food, home, gas, vehicle, furniture, job, shoes or clothes? We all depend upon the efforts of others. You may pay or trade for those items, but does that mean you should not appreciate the fact you didn't have to grow your own vegetables and raise your own cattle? Does that mean you shouldn't appreciate that you don't have to walk to work because others supply the economy with cars and gas? What about your job? You give 100%. You work hard to deserve your job. But is any job totally safe, even to top performers? You only have to read the newspaper to know the answer to that question is no. Oscar Wilde once said, "The best way to appreciate your job is to imagine yourself without one." Isn't that the truth! Just as the employer owes gratitude to his employee, so the employee owes gratitude to his employer. It is always, always, always a two-way street.

We know that some may be so overwhelmed with the day-to-day of living they simply do not feel they have the capacity to see any goodness in their lives. Some who may be economically stressed believe they simply have nothing to be grateful for. But, your perception creates your reality. Alphonse Karr said, "Some people are always grumbling because roses have thorns; I am thankful that thorns have roses." You have both roses and thorns in your life. Which do you see?

According to Doc Childre and Howard Martin, authors of *The HeartMath Solution*, "When you're in the grip of frustration, love can seem pretty much out of the question. Care is going to be a stretch. But appreciation is easy—even if it starts out kind of snide like, 'I appreciate the fact I haven't fallen flat on my face…

yet.' After a couple of stabs at it, you're going to stumble across one that sincerely touches you. Maybe it's your friends, your partner, your loved ones. One strong dose of appreciation can turn your perceptions around 180 degrees."

Gratitude is one among many emotions, like love and kindness, that we can give and give and give, and no matter how much we give, from the day we are born until the day we die, we will never run out. Genuine gratitude creates a cycle, but it does have to start somewhere. It can start with you. ❦

❦

What if you gave someone a gift,
and they neglected to thank you for it —
would you be likely
to give them another?
Life is the same way.
In order to attract more of the blessings
that life has to offer,
you must truly appreciate
what you already have.

— RALPH MARSTON

CHAPTER 4

༶

Gratitude and the Law of Attraction

*Be thankful for what you have
and you will end up having more.
But if you concentrate
on what you don't have,
you'll never, ever have enough.*

—OPRAH WINFREY

What does gratitude have to do with the Law of Attraction? Well, according to the Law of Attraction, you will have that which you think about most. According to Prentice Mulford, one of the earliest pioneers of the New Thought teaching,

> Everything that's coming into your life you are attracting into your life. And it's attracted to you by virtue of the images you're holding in your mind. It's what you're thinking. Whatever is going on in your mind you are attracting to you.

Bob Doyle, author and Law of Attraction Specialist, also tells us that:

The law of attraction doesn't care whether you perceive something to be good or bad, or whether you don't want it or whether you do want it. It's responding to your thoughts. So if you're looking at a mountain of debt, feeling terrible about it, that's the signal you're putting out into the Universe. 'I feel really bad because of all this debt I've got.' You're just affirming it to yourself. You feel it on every level of your being. That's what you're going to get more of.

In his book, *Beach Money*, Jordan Adler writes about his struggle to become an entrepreneur and then to become a successful entrepreneur. Jordan shares many stories of his life that highlight great financial difficulties and numerous failed starts. Jordan tells us that his life changed when his thoughts changed. It started with feeling lucky. As Jordan points out, many of us believe that lucky people "get all the luck." One day, Jordan was told "You have a star following you." He interpreted that as meaning he had a "LUCKY" star following him, and his entire attitude changed. He *felt* lucky and noticed that he "began to get all the luck!" He felt that his "luck changed overnight." Every day something lucky happened to him… a promotion, a pay raise, meeting all the right people. He saw himself as a "magnet for good things." Here is what Jordan says about this:

> This may sound like hocus-pocus, but here's my explanation. When you see yourself as unlucky (or whatever negative word you use to describe yourself), your subconscious mind begins to look for and find evidence that supports that belief. We all want to be right. I'm not a

psychologist, but I do know that we attract what we think about! If you identify yourself as successful and really believe it, you'll begin to attract success. If you see yourself as fun, you'll begin to attract fun! Your subconscious mind will actually draw to you that which is consistent with whom you know yourself to be!

According to the Law of Attraction, as you think, so you will be and so you will have. Also, keep in mind that thinking in terms of what you don't want will neither keep the bad at bay nor will it bring to you the good things you want. Rather, you must think in terms of wanting good things and noticing and reflecting on the good things that already exist in your life. Good and bad cannot co-exist in the same place in your mind.

> Gratitude for the abundance
> you have received
> is the best insurance
> that the abundance will continue.
> — MUHAMMAD

In her book *Gratitude: Affirming the Good Things in Life*, Melody Beattie talked about the affects of deprived thinking and her first experience with gratitude. All her life, Melody had dreamed of being married with a family and a beautiful home. She did get married, and after her first child was born, she and her husband bought a home. Unfortunately, Melody did not see her new home as beautiful. She writes: "It had been used as rental property for fifteen years and had been standing vacant for a year. Now it was three stories of broken windows and broken wood. Some rooms had ten layers of wallpaper on the walls. Some walls had holes straight through to the outdoors. The floors were covered with bright orange carpeting with large stains." It was all they could afford, and they had neither the money nor the skills to fix the house.

While others saw her as lucky, for months all Melody could do was cry about her ugly home. One day, Melody was fortunate to find the answer within herself. She decided, as a last ditch effort, to try gratitude. She gave thanks to God for everything—for the layers of peeling wallpaper and everything else she hated about the house. For every negative thought that entered her mind, she countered it with a grateful one. After several months of forcing this ritual upon herself, Melody changed her attitude and "started taking care of the house as though it were a dream home." It was a lot of work, but with a new attitude, Melody became energized and creative and eventually fixed up their dilapidated house and turned it into a beautiful home. She learned about textured paint to hide flaws. She bought flawed furniture and covered the flaws with lace doilies. She tackled the problem of missing kitchen cabinet doors by removing all the doors and enjoying the new look of an open country kitchen. When she concentrated on, and lamented over what appeared ugly, there was no room in her mind to envision the beauty under all the layers of old carpet and unattractive wallpaper. With a new attitude of gratitude, however, Melody drew into her life an abundance of answers and beauty.

The Law of Attraction has received a lot of renewed interest and press in recent years. Some believe and some do not believe. Some have experienced its truth. We believe the Law of Attraction began with lessons from God. We need only point to the story of Job to know gratitude and faith can overcome the worst of evils. First, we learn from Job that what is feared becomes what is real. "For the thing which I greatly feared is come upon me, and that which I was afraid of is come unto me." Job 3:25. We later learn from Job that faith and gratitude can turn one's life around.

༜

*I find that the more willing I am to be grateful
for the small things in life,
the bigger stuff just seems to show up
from unexpected sources,
and I am constantly looking forward
to each day with all the surprises
that keep coming my way!*
— LOUISE L. HAY

Throughout the Bible we find evidence confirming that which we think will come to pass. First, according to Philippians 4:8, "whatsoever things are true, whatsoever things are honest, whatsoever things are just, whatsoever things are pure, whatsoever things are lovely, whatsoever things are of good report; if there be any virtue, and if there be any praise, think on these things." Then, "as he thinketh in his heart, so is he." Proverbs 23:7.

Melodie Beattie talked about using affirmations like this:

> Using affirmations means replacing negative messages with positive ones. We change what we say so we can change what we see. If we emphasize and empower the good in ourselves, we will see and get more of that. If we empower the good in others, we will get more of that, too.

We both wear wristbands that say "Thoughts become things, choose the good ones," (a phrase coined by Mike Dooley, author of Notes from the Universe and Infinite Possibilities, tut.com). This is what we believe to be the truth as originally told in the Bible. We wear the wristbands to remind us to think about the good and also to do good, such as feeling and expressing gratitude in our lives.

In Luke we were taught "love ye your enemies, and do good, and lend, hoping for nothing again; and your reward shall be great, and ye shall be the children of the Highest." Luke 6:35. We also have been taught, "Be not deceived; God is not mocked; for whatsoever a man soweth, that shall he also reap. For he that soweth to his flesh shall of the flesh reap corruption; but he that soweth to the Spirit shall of the Spirit reap life everlasting. And let us not be weary in well doing; for in due season we shall reap, if we faint not." Galatians 6:7-9. In these lessons we learn first that our gratitude should be unconditional and without limits or expectations. We also learn that what we think and how we live will determine our bounty.

Debbie grew up in what she describes as, "on the lower end of middle class." Her father was a carpenter and her mother worked in banks, first as a teller and eventually working her way up to "the floor." Debbie writes about the important role gratitude has played in her life:

> I lived in New York State for most of my youth. Growing up, although we weren't poor, we never had a lot of money for extras. My parents didn't make a lot of money, but my parents worked hard, planned carefully and were resilient. For example, after my mother received a small inheritance, my parents decided to use the money for a home. My mother was pregnant with me, but that didn't stop her and my father from laboring together nights and weekends to build the house our family would live in for the next 14 years.
>
> From time to time, my father would be out of work, either because of the economy or the weather, but my parents always made ends meet. There were lots of things I wanted but didn't have, but there was also lots of things I had that I didn't need. As I grew up and left the family home, I had my own financial struggles, often working just to pay the bills. I couldn't always go out with my friends, and I never had the wardrobe some of my friends had. I was 28 when I bought my first home—a 1,000 square foot villa. Many times I would just look around my home and feel I was the luckiest person in the world, because I had so much—a job I enjoyed, a beautiful home

and a family I loved! I didn't have a ton of extras and I didn't have a home that would ever grace the covers of *House Beautiful,* but I had everything I needed and everything I had gave me joy. My Mom helped me find my home, bought me a television set and other extras and nurtured my soul; and my Dad built shelves, helped me hang wallpaper and fixed anything that broke. I also had wonderful neighbors. I remember asking my Dad once, 'when will I get to the point when I won't need my parents to help me anymore?!' My dear father passed away in 1998 but left me with a legacy of love and appreciation. My wonderful mother is still alive and still giving to her children.

As my life has progressed, my blessings continued to grow. I was fortunate to follow a dream of going to law school after a 10-year career as a paralegal. I met my husband there, married him in 2000 and then worked side-by-side with him to build our home. I've moved quite a bit, living in some terrific places. Most recently, my husband and I moved away from Connecticut and took two years off from work to cruise the East Coast of the United States, Bermuda and the Bahamas on our sailboat. Now that we are returning to land and to work, many of our friends are feeling sorry for us, but I see this as an opportunity for our next adventure and I'm very excited that we are ending up in a town entirely new to me!

My life, much like everyone else's, was not all perfect. There were times of sadness and tears and disappointments, times when I doubted myself, times when I suffered great loss and times when I was horribly lonely. As a whole, however, I have always felt that the gifts in my life were plentiful and not to be taken for granted. I am where I want to be at this moment and so I am grateful for everything I have experienced so far—even the bad and the ugly—because all that has passed brought me to this present moment. Will my life continue to be blessed? I know the answer to that question depends on me and whether I stay focused on the blessings that are already in my life.

Can we move mountains? You bet! That power is truly within us. Mark taught us that "whoever shall say unto this mountain, 'Be thou removed, and be thou cast into the sea;' and shall not doubt in his heart, but shall believe that those things which he saith shall come to pass; he shall have whatsoever he saith." Mark 11:23

One of the most vivid examples of the Law of Attraction in Peggy's life is her dog, Leiden. Here's how she describes what happened:

> I am a dog lover, well, perhaps better said, an animal lover. I already had four dogs but wanted what I call a "holding dog"—one that could sit in my lap, be a pampered princess, and come to work with me everyday. I did my research and determined the perfect dog would

be a female Papillon who was a couple of years old and less than ten pounds. I started my search on the animal rescue sites looking for just the right dog. I made an application to one rescue organization that rejected me because of their policy not to adopt to multiple dog households. So, I kept looking. I contacted several other rescue organizations. I wasn't having any luck finding my perfect dog.

Then, one day, I was having lunch with a friend at a local restaurant. I was describing in great detail my ideal dog. Moments later, a lady approached my table, handed me a note with her phone number written on it and announced, "I have your dog. I overhead you talking and I believe I have just what you are looking for. Please call me if you think you might be interested." Call her?! I wanted to know if I could follow her home—and I did. There she introduced me to Leiden, my now constant companion for more than four years. She was exactly what I described—a three-year-old female Papillon, weighing less than ten pounds—perfect!

We believe in the Law of Attraction. If you tell the Universe what you want, if you believe you can have it, and if you are grateful every day for the blessings already in your life, miracles can and will happen.

You were given the wonderful power to choose your own thoughts. It is only you who can choose whether your thoughts will be about good things or bad. Use your power and the Law of

Attraction to bring into your life all the good things you want. Choose good thoughts—push away any negative thoughts by replacing them with good ones. When Peggy experiences negative thoughts or emotions, she says her favorite affirmation, "I'm whole, perfect, strong, powerful, loving, harmonious, happy, healthy, wealthy, wise and grateful." And so she is.

Choose to be grateful for each and every blessing in your life, from your relationship with God to your relationship with family and friends; from the rain that nourishes the earth to the sun that warms your heart; from the dog that greets you after a long day at work to the fact you have a job; from the opportunity to spend time with a grandchild to the flowers you never noticed before on your drive to the store. Just as the lucky have all the luck, so the grateful will have all the blessings!

CHAPTER 5

ෲ

Finding the Gratitude Within

*If only people who worry about
their liabilities would think about
the riches they do possess,
they would stop worrying.
Would you sell both your eyes
for a million dollars... or your legs...
or your hands... or your hearing?
Add up what you do have,
and you'll find that you won't sell them
for all the gold in the world.
The best things in life are yours,
if you can appreciate yourself.*

— DALE CARNEGIE

The ability to appreciate or have gratitude for your circumstances is not always an easy task. It may not come naturally to you for any number of reasons. Present circumstances, for example, may be such that you are just too busy or too stressed. We live in a hectic world and with so many things happening, often at the same time, it is indeed rare when we can stop for even a moment to really savor and appreciate the pleasant things in our lives.

It seems like technology has contributed to our busy-ness. And, it was supposed to save us time so we would have time for the things that are really important. Remember when the newest technology was the fax machine? Debbie was working as a paralegal at the time, and what she remembers most is that it ultimately meant a faster work pace and more stress—everybody had to have everything right away, simply because they could! Today's technology is more advanced than most of us ever imagined it would be, but have those advancements contributed to making our lives more stressful? We wear invisible leashes that tether us to our technology—our email, our texting, our cell phones. We are more accessible to others than ever before, and as a result, others are demanding we be more accessible. Whatever the cause or causes, we seem to have less time, yet more demands on our time, with everybody seemingly wanting everything yesterday!

For some, it may be you were raised in a culture or environment where showing appreciation was simply not the custom. Regardless of whether it is time, temperament or circumstances or something else that has become your obstacle to attaining growth, joy and success through gratitude, you are not alone. When we randomly asked people we know to name some things for which they were grateful, many people had to think long and hard before having an answer. Some would struggle and then come up with a few things and then somehow the conversation turned back around to the negatives in their life. We simply are not in the habit of focusing on the positives, and certainly not on a daily basis.

What this means is that almost all of us struggle every day to find time to get our tasks done. We move from one day into the next, just happy we were able to hold it together for one more day. When we think about tomorrow, our only hope is that we can make it through. So how are we going to fit in one more thing to do... finding the gratitude within ourselves? Before we answer that question, let's take a moment to recognize the constants that surround us every day.

EXERCISE FOUR: *Since you are reading this book, you are likely in a place where you are comfortable and/or have some extra time. Take the time you have now to think about your life as it is at this moment. Think first about the people in your life—your family and friends in particular. Bring to mind as many family members and friends as you can and as you think of each one, think of at least one positive attribute of each person. Take your time doing this so you can really connect with your feelings for each person. Now think about your home. If you are home, get up and walk through each room. If you are somewhere else, make the walk in your mind. As you go into each room, make note of what you have. Think about how it feels to be home and what you like to do when you are home. Do you like to listen to music or play the piano? Do you like to play in the yard with your spouse or children? Cook? Entertain? Exercise? Read the newspaper while enjoying a cup of coffee or tea? Try to remember and even re-experience some of the activities you have enjoyed in your home. When you look around each room, look not only at the objects, but consider the memories associated with those objects and the activities you have enjoyed in that room. Again, try not to do this exercise quickly or abstractly. It can take time to unlock to the memories within.*

When your mind is filled with warm thoughts of your loved ones and memories you care most about...

Now imagine it's all gone... your family... your friends... your home... all that helps hold your memories... and all that would be a part of your future memories. Undoubtedly this is not a place you want to be!

Now, remember that you do still have these precious people and these precious memories. Feel better? This is where the road to finding the gratitude within yourself can begin!

For those of us who have experienced an actual loss, perhaps through the death of a loved one or the destruction of home or the loss or theft of an heirloom or other treasured item. With our mourning, we likely also experienced some level of appreciation for what we no longer have.

Debbie lost her dear father almost 11 years ago. It was not a sudden event and so there was some time for reflection before her father passed on. Debbie remembers feeling, as she drove nearly every night first to the hospital and then to the nursing home where her father was eventually under hospice care, that there were so many, many things in life that now seemed meaningless but somehow had been elevated to important; and there were so many, many things in life that were important but had been relegated to the back seat. The only thing that seemed really important anymore was one more opportunity, every day, to spend cherished time with her father. This is what happens when we experience loss: priorities change and we vow to stay focused on the important things.

Imagining loss is merely an exercise to try to help us see how our life is truly blessed—a reminder, if you will, of what money can't buy and that nothing lasts forever. We are inspired to value what is still present but perhaps previously obscured. We begin to learn to appreciate.

> Live your life so that the fear of death
> can never enter your heart.
> When you arise in the morning,
> give thanks for the morning light.
> Give thanks for your life
> and strength.
> Give thanks for your food
> and for the joy of living.
> And if perchance you see
> no reason for giving thanks,
> rest assured the fault is in yourself.
>
> —CHIEF TECUMSEH, SHAWNEE INDIAN CHIEF

If you experienced gratitude during Exercise Four, the next step is making it a habit. But, again, how do we do that with our busy and stressful lives?! Frankly, when it comes to finding what is special in your life, you will discover it really doesn't require a major modification of your schedule. You won't have to try to "fit it in." You won't have to set aside an hour to reflect on your life, although you can if you want to. All you really need is one moment… as many times a day as you can spare… to move toward making gratitude a habit.

We know bad habits are hard to break. We have learned that good habits are also hard to create! We asked our husbands to participate with us in sharing three gratitude expressions each day. At first it was awkward and difficult. We are so used to talking with our spouses about daily problems and difficulties. We don't know how it happens, but we tend to use our spouses as sounding boards for gripes and complaints. It's like newspapers printing only bad news. Can you imagine how you might feel if you picked up the paper today and found that most of the stories focused on what was good and right in the world and your community? Don't you love reading those human interest stories that tell about one person helping another? Those stories let us know there are some really terrific people in our world, and we want to read more of those stories. We can't change what the newspapers write, but we did want to change the focus in our lives from the negatives to the positives.

We persisted every day with our gratitude expressions, and it did get easier. Eventually it became a natural part of our day. Every night, as the day winds down, we take a few minutes to reflect with our spouses about what happened or what we noticed that we were grateful for that day. It takes 21 days to develop a new habit—do this for 21 days with a spouse, partner or friend, and you may have a new habit for life!

Making a habit of finding gratitude in yourself can be as simple as noticing what seems to be the smallest and simplest things in life. For example, since you are reading this book, you either had the money to purchase it or maybe someone loaned it to you or gave it to you as a gift. Maybe you borrowed it from the library. If you bought it, perhaps you can appreciate having a few extra dollars to purchase something for your own enjoyment. If someone loaned or gave it to you, perhaps you can appreciate that someone values you enough to spend their few extra dollars on you or cares enough about you to share something inspirational. You see how this works? If you borrowed it from the library, you can appreciate _____ (you fill in the blank).

EXERCISE FIVE: From the moment you rise in the morning to the moment you close your eyes to sleep, there are innumerable opportunities for appreciation, even if it's just the flowers blooming in your neighbor's garden! The moment you open your eyes tomorrow, start looking for those opportunities. Don't get out of bed until you find at least one! You don't have to be creative or smart or educated or spiritual. You only have to open your eyes and your heart, and you only need take one moment... as many times a day as you can spare. Tomorrow do the same. The next day, and the next day, and the next day, do the same.

A good friend sent Debbie an email with a summary of a fascinating story that ran in the *Washington Post* some time ago. Here is the short version of what was reported:

At a Washington DC Metro Station on a cold Friday morning during rush hour in January 2007, a violinist played six classical pieces for 43 minutes. In that time approximately 1,100 people passed by, most of them on their way to work.

After three minutes a middle-aged man noticed there was a musician playing. He slowed his pace and stopped for a few seconds and then hurried to meet his schedule.

At four minutes, the violinist received his first dollar—a woman threw the money in the till and, without stopping, continued to walk.

At six minutes, a young man leaned against the wall to listen, then looked at his watch and started to walk again.

At ten minutes, a three-year-old-boy stopped, but his mother tugged him along hurriedly. He kept trying to watch the violinist. Finally, the mother pushed hard and the child continued to walk, turning his head all the time. This action was repeated by several other children. Every parent, without exception, forced them to move on.

At 43 minutes, the musician stopped playing. Only seven people had stopped and stayed for a while. Twenty-seven had given him money but had also continued to walk their normal pace. He collected $32 and change.

The anonymous violinist was Joshua Bell, one of the finest classical musicians in the world. During that cold rush-hour morning in January 2007 at the Metro in Washington, D.C., he played some of the most intricate masterpieces ever written, with a violin worth $3.5 million dollars. Two days prior, Joshua Bell sold out a theater in Boston where the average seat was $100. Nonetheless, only two people had recognized his talent and only one person had recognized him. Otherwise, nobody applauded and nobody really noticed. Some later didn't even remember a musician. Some were visibly annoyed at the intrusion.

The Washington Post reported this story as part of a social experiment about perception, taste and people's priorities. The questions raised were: In a common place environment at an inappropriate hour, do we perceive beauty? Do we stop to appreciate it? Do we recognize talent in an unexpected context?

One possible conclusion reached from this experiment could be: If we do not have a moment to stop and listen to one of the best musicians in the world playing some of the finest music ever written, with one of the most beautiful instruments… how many other beautiful things are we missing?

The first step toward making gratitude a habit can seem tough and useless, especially today. These are trying times! For many, it's hard to find and keep a job, build a business, get health care, pay the mortgage! Remember, some of our friends had to really think about it when we asked them for gratitude expressions, but nobody says you can't start small and build from there, one step at a time. When you consider that you might be the next person to come across a Joshua Bell, don't you want to be the person who not only notices, but stops, listens and appreciates?

Remember, too, that feelings of gratitude do not necessarily always come from a good deed or a kindness. Sometimes the things we are grateful for are born out of a hard lesson learned! When Debbie was in her 20's, she was lured with the promise of a free gift to hear a sales pitch about a camping membership that was developed to be much like a timeshare. Besides what then seemed like a cool gift, the product itself brought back warm memories of great family outings. The pitch was persuasive and Debbie signed up on the spot. This is what she writes about it and the lesson she learned:

My family lived in New York until I was 14. As long as I can remember, our family vacations were spent camping during the first two weeks of August. Initially my parents rented a pop-up camper that my Dad had to crank open. We graduated to an automated pop-up and then my parents eventually bought a small travel trailer that Dad pulled behind his pick-up truck. The day we made that purchase is as vivid in my memory as yesterday. I loved those camping trips! We had great family time and we saw much of the great outdoors, from caves and caverns to zoos and parks and more. One of my favorite trips was when we went to Myrtle Beach and stayed in a campground right on the beach. My sister loved the ocean and I loved the pool, and so you can imagine we were both in the water all day every day!

With these great memories in tow, I was a sucker to be had when my Mom and I headed for my appointment to hear the sales pitch for the camping membership. All I had to ask was "where do I sign?" Since I couldn't pay in full, I financed it over several years. In addition to that payment, I also had to pay an annual maintenance fee for as long as I owned the membership. Well, I wasn't a kid anymore, we didn't take family vacations, and the novelty quickly wore off. I never really used the membership. So I paid it off, which in total cost me thousands of dollars, and then I decided to just give it up so I wouldn't have to continue paying the annual fees for something I no longer wanted and felt foolish for buying in the first place.

I had fantastic childhood memories of camping with my family, but the reality was that camping was not in my *future*, so I cut my losses and let it go. I'm not sure what is more embarrassing—losing that much money or losing it for what seems now to be a silly purchase. Nonetheless, I learned a hard but good lesson. I would never again buy anything of that magnitude on the spot. In fact, I have learned that with most non-ordinary purchases, if I allow myself to mull it over, I find either that I don't want the product or I find something better or more to my liking. I am never going to be happy that I lost that money on the camping membership, but I am *grateful* for the lesson I learned from it. I believe that experience made me more cautious about my purchases. I am also *grateful* that the lesson I needed to learn did not come at a higher cost. It certainly could have been worse.

So it is not only the so-called happy times that can inspire us toward gratitude. Think also about the lessons you have learned in life and how you learned them.

CR

> There are no mistakes, no coincidences.
> All events are blessings
> given to us to learn from.
> — ELISABETH KUBLER-ROSS

Maybe you have your own "camping membership" story. The key is not to lament over the loss or mistake, but to learn and grow from it and then to let it go and be grateful for the lesson! Every opportunity for growth is something to be grateful for, no matter the circumstance. Debbie's very dear friends, Bob and Ruth Riebel, gave her a beautiful Successories plaque many years ago that she continues to treasure and hang in her home. It says "Every obstacle is a stepping stone to your success." She truly believes that. You can learn to be grateful for everything that brings you a smile, love, friendship and growth, whether in the form of a kindness or an obstacle.

After Exercise Five, did you notice any changes within yourself? Does life seem to be more enjoyable? Does life seem to move a little slower because you are appreciating the little things more? Do you find yourself smiling more? Feeling happier? Being more patient? Has the impulse to thank somebody you never would have thanked before crept into your heart? If any of those are true, your habit is taking root. What starts as a habit can turn into a way of life—an enjoyable and rewarding way of life.

Next, let's cultivate our gratitude through the expression of gratitude. To cultivate is to foster the growth of something. By sharing your feelings of gratitude with others, you can grow the joy not only in the lives of others but in your own life as well.

EXERCISE SIX: *Today, thank someone for something, even if you think it is ordinary. In fact, thank everybody for everything! Thank your assistant for making the coffee in your office. Thank your spouse for emptying the dishwasher or taking out the trash or cleaning the toilet. Thank the bagger at your grocery store. Even if someone did something to aggravate you today, find something to thank him or her* *for. Did your son forget to take out the trash? Well, isn't there at least one thing you can thank him for today? Maybe he worked hard at school or work. Maybe he made his bed this morning or put his shoes away or walked the dog, even if you had to ask. Maybe he's sorry about the trash... now that's something to really be thankful for! Tomorrow thank someone else. Do the same thing each day following. There are a zillion things to thank people for!*

Our experience has been that kindness generally begets kindness. We also believe that gratitude also begets kindness. These are building blocks for enduring relationships. When Debbie bought her house in Orlando, she kept her trash cans on the side of her house. Her neighbor knew she didn't like the way her trash cans looked from the street, but she didn't really know how to solve the problem herself. Recognizing the need, one day her neighbor took some extra fence pieces he had, recruited his brother who also lived in the neighborhood, and installed the fence in such a way so as to hide the trash cans from the street. When Debbie got home from work that day, she was overwhelmed with gratitude. What a nice thing to do! Some time later her neighbor asked if he could put his satellite dish in one of her trees as he didn't have any that were high enough. She happily said "Sure!" Her neighbors were now grateful to her. This is community! This is being connected. People are doing kind things for you all the time. Wait until you see what happens, not only to the people you appreciate, but to you and your relationships when you make a habit of recognizing kindness with gratitude!

To educate yourself for the
feeling of gratitude means to take
nothing for granted, but to always
seek out and value the kindness
that stands behind the action.
Nothing that is done for you
is a matter of course.
Everything originates in a will
for the good, which is directed at you.
Train yourself never to put off the word or
action for the expression of gratitude.

ALBERT SCHWEITZER

CHAPTER 6

ॐ

Making Gratitude Your Attitude

*A positive attitude may not
solve all your problems,
but it will annoy enough people
to make it worth the effort.*

— HERM ALBRIGHT

By now, you are probably getting the hang of this appreciation and gratitude thing. You are probably noticing even the smallest things in life that can make you happy, and you probably are happier. One of the greatest rewards of appreciating what is around us is that we end up happy! We recognize the abundance in our lives and we become filled with a positive energy that radiates out, makes other people happy and then returns to us ten-fold.

If you have started to get into the habit of gratitude, let's boost into overdrive and develop our habit of gratitude into an attitude of gratitude! Attitude is a feeling or emotion we hold toward a fact or state. Winston Churchill said, "Attitude is a little thing that makes a big difference."

One of the wonderful things about life is that we can control our attitude—we *can* control our feelings and emotions. Some people may tell you they "can't." We think "can't" is one of the ugliest words in our vocabulary—usually it's a self-fulfilling prophesy! If *you* don't control your feelings and emotions, who does? And how did *they* get control? Was it wrestled away from you? Did someone steal it in the night? When we feel out of control, it's probably because we are *letting* someone or something else *be* in control. Imagine you are the only person on earth—would you be in control of your own feelings and emotions then? Just because there are other people in the world doesn't mean you can't control your feelings and emotions. When it comes to how you feel and how you think, you *can* choose to be in control and you *can* choose a positive attitude of gratitude. As the *Nike* commercials say, "Just do it!"

If you have already experienced the joy and positive energy that comes with appreciation, you have probably realized that your positive energy simply cannot be contained. You have probably already started sharing it with others, and maybe it has come back to you, too. If you haven't yet ventured to share, try this:

EXERCISE SEVEN: *Every day, identify at least three things you are grateful for and share your gratitude affirmations with someone you care about. Try to get your sharing partner to do the same—to share with you three things they are grateful for that day. Don't be too tough on your sharing partner at first. Just as it may have taken a while for you to get comfortable doing this, it may take him or her some time as well. If you feel like you don't have anyone to share this exercise with, you can do it alone—just write your three things down on a piece of paper or in a journal, and reflect on the abundance in your life.*

When we started this project, we asked—okay, we pleaded and cajoled—our husbands to participate with us in this exercise. Some of you can probably appreciate what we went through. We heard "that's silly" or "that's too touchy-feely for me" or "I don't have time" or "I can't think of anything." We love our husbands, but whew, our job was cut out for us. Aside from the fact that for many people, this just is not a part of their everyday world, it's probably less so for men. Peggy's husband likes to joke that he lives a "groundhog life"—every day is exactly the same. Their daily gratitude exercise has helped him appreciate the variety in his life and has given him a different perspective.

Women seem to look for opportunities for spiritual, mental and emotional self-improvement. Most men—but not all—not so much. They were taught their responsibility was to go out and work and provide for the family. The woman is typically the nurturer and the "touchy-feely" half of the relationship. Feeling and expressing gratitude just does not seem to fit the macho persona! Well, it's a bit like that in our families. Nonetheless, we are nothing if not persistent… and truth be told, our guys support our efforts at personal development and did participate with us. In fact, our guys are even starting to get used to this gratitude expression thing and we think doing this exercise with our spouses has brought more joy to our relationships.

Not to slight men, women can have their struggles with the effort toward gratitude, too. We both sometimes have to work a little harder to find something positive in the day, and so it is good to have our spouses to encourage us as well. Every day we have a focused conversation with our spouses on the positives of our daily journey. How bad can that be?! For at least a few minutes every day, we are dedicated to sharing something positive with each other. As a result, we have infused more positive energy into our relationship, which means there is less room for negative thoughts and energy. Doing this every day has now become more natural for all of us, even the guys. In fact, if it happens that we don't bring it up, sometimes our guys start the conversation or wonder why we haven't, because now they are thinking about it every day!

We all want to be happy. But, sometimes we don't know how to start and sometimes it is hard to be positive all the time by yourself, especially if there are people around you who don't yet get how great it is to be positive and are still stuck in a negative world. That's why it's so fun to enlist someone else to join you in your gratitude affirmations every day. Find any like-minded friend or relative who will spend a few minutes every day talking with you about the good things that are happening in your lives. You will find that you inspire each other!

If you are still wondering who and what we should be appreciating, why put a limit on it? Thank everybody for everything! Debbie appreciated the cable guy when he came and fixed a sporadic internet connection, *and* he was most pleasant about it, *and* he followed up to make sure her family was satisfied, so she sent a note to his employer. Debbie and her husband, Craig, were cruising for two years on their sailboat, which can make handling the administrative side of one's personal life difficult. One agent handled most of their insurance needs, and one person in particular in her agent's office took care of any issue that would arise. Not only was she responsive and a "get-the-job-done" kind of person, but she also has the best personality and attitude! When Debbie and Craig returned to land, Debbie sent her a card telling her how much she appreciated all the help she gave them while they were cruising and a few weeks later called her to invite her for lunch just to say thanks again.

Anytime anybody does anything for you, no matter how small or seemingly insignificant, and no matter if it's "part of their job," they deserve appreciation! Whether it's your neighbor, the person who works for your insurance agent, the person who cuts your grass, your employee or your customer, everyone craves… and deserves… appreciation.

There really are no boundaries to gratitude. The more you feel it, the more you'll feel it. When you feel gratitude for someone or something and you express it, it not only makes the other person feel good, it makes you feel good, too. We all like to feel good. And what do we end up doing when we experience something that makes us feel good? We look for more of it! Do you like ice cream? If you do, you probably have it at least occasionally. It tastes good and it's fun to eat. We are happy when we see an ice cream store! So what do we do? We eat more ice cream! It's the same with gratitude and appreciation. We start finding more and more to appreciate because appreciation creates positive energy that makes us feel good! When we are appreciating everybody and everything and feeling good, we are happy and our happiness is totally contagious.

In mid-2009, Debbie attended a networking conference for women in business hosted by an organization called WOAMTEC (Women on a Mission to Earn Commission). There were about

250 women there. Debbie had heard about the organization, had attended one luncheon as a guest and was interested in learning more and possibly becoming a member. She did not know a single other person at the conference, but what she experienced was unforgettable and she signed up as a member before she left.

The positive energy started at that WOAMTEC conference when Debbie encountered a group of happy, laughing women entering the hosting hotel and she inquired where they were from. It turned out they were from the chapter she was interested in joining! It only got better from there. It was amazing, because everybody was happy! How could that be? Nobody screened these women for positive energy, and nobody was excluded. The invitation didn't say "Come only if you have no problems in your life." In fact, at Debbie's lunch table, to her right sat a woman who had lost her 16-year-old nephew to an accident two weeks before, and to her left sat a woman who had lost her brother to an accident four months before! How is it that 250 women from all walks of life and with varying issues in their lives (we all have them!) ended up in the same place generating so much enthusiasm and positive energy?

It started a year and a half prior with the vision of WOAMTEC's founder, Kathleen Hawkins, who dreamed of creating an organization where women could appreciate, inspire, encourage and support other women in business. The seed started with Kathleen, who continues to inspire the group, but it has spread from one woman to another, and there is no limit in sight! When we inspire others to happiness, they inspire others, and it returns to us! You create the cycle of your life… choose to make it positive and you will see remarkable change within yourself and your life. Debbie was so inspired that she has become an Executive Director and has launched a new chapter of WOAMTEC in Sarasota, Florida!

We know life has its difficulties—its twists and unexpected turns—just like for the two women at Debbie's lunch table. Sometimes those difficulties feel so overwhelming and insurmountable that we lack the ability to accept inspiration from others. In those times of difficulty, especially when it seems we are at our lowest, it can be helpful to look back to good times and take our inspiration from our past. But let's face it, in tough times, it's hard to remember the good times. Having a gratitude journal can help, because it allows you to document a record to yourself that will be a reminder of the good times and an inspiration through the bad times. Remember, "When the going gets tough—the tough get going!" We know you can accomplish this.

EXERCISE EIGHT: *Start a gratitude journal by writing every day about something or someone you are grateful for. Consider it a short note to yourself—just a sentence or two. You will not only feel good, but you are now creating a record of the joys in your life. When times are bad, we have to remember there were also good times. We have created a Gratitude Expressions journal that makes it easy to look back on past joys. In our five-year journal, each page represents five years of the same day, so every day when you write in your journal, the entry above is your entry on the same day from the prior year. It's fun and inspiring to look back on a positive moment from the same day on a prior year, and our journal makes that easy. So every day, you are writing about a present joy and you are looking back at past joys—happiness on top of happiness! Then, when something bad happens in your life—and we all have those times—looking back at the good times can help us realize that good times can and do exist!*

After doing these exercises consistently over time, you may find your outlook and your demeanor changing. Debbie has been sharing the gratitude expressions with her husband for several months and finds she is more patient and understanding. By concentrating on the good things, not only is she happier, she feels she has attracted more positive energy into her life. She has become better able to deal with negative energy, which now mostly comes from others. Debbie has also noticed a continual growth in her relationship with her husband!

Don't be surprised if you discover that your new positive attitude attracts others to you—like bugs to a light bulb. People like to be around positive people who love and appreciate themselves and everything around them. You may also find you are no longer interested in exposing yourself to negative people and negative events. Both Peggy and Debbie have mostly given up reading the newspaper and listening to television news—there just isn't anything positive the media is willing to report. Wouldn't it be great if only good news was reported?! We believe everyone would have a different outlook and the results would be contagious.

While we all deal with issues or problems that crop up, either in our lives or in the lives of friends and other loved ones, the more time we spend appreciating, the less time we have to spend complaining. The end result… an attitude of gratitude that equips us with a greater ability to get through anything! ❧

CHAPTER 7

✼

Expressing Gratitude

*Feeling gratitude
and not expressing it
is like wrapping a present
and not giving it.*

— WILLIAM ARTHUR WARD

Here's a trick question. Is expressing gratitude important? Some might think so, but others may be scratching their head. Even simply saying "thank you" does not come easily for some people, but that's okay. Life is a learning process. We weren't born knowing much. We don't know anyone who was born knowing how to tie a shoelace or calculate algebraic equations or drive a car. It's okay to admit we have some things to learn, because we all do; and because we are all in different situations, we learn different things at different times. For those who have difficulty saying "thank you," maybe you see it as a sign of weakness or maybe you were simply never taught the significance or importance of showing appreciation.

If today is the first day you are going to attempt to express gratitude to another person, and all you do is say "thank you" one time to one person, job well done! Those two words can change a person's day. Several years ago, Debbie was checking out of a department store. When the cashier handed her the receipt and package, Debbie said a very simple, "Thank you." The cashier stopped and looked at Debbie with a puzzled look and said, "Nobody has ever said thank you to me in this job before." Isn't that amazing?! How could that be? How do you think that cashier felt, receiving that one "thank you"? It must have had some effect on her, because she stopped what she was doing, looked Debbie in the eye and responded. Our guess is it probably affected her in a good way. It costs absolutely nothing to say "thank you" and yet the reward is immeasurable.

We don't know if Debbie's "thank you" changed that cashier's day, but it sure had an impact on Debbie. It's funny how the mind works. What an odd memory to retain. That event actually happened more than "several" years ago. It was more like 25 years ago, and it happened at the Zayre's store in Sanford, Florida. That store is long gone and the event lasted only a few seconds, but for some reason, it was significant enough to Debbie that she has remembered it all these years. For her, though, it was not the fact of maybe making someone's day that created the staying power of that memory. Rather, it was the fact that nobody had ever said "thank you" to this young girl. We think that is profoundly sad. If you feel the same, we know together we can make a difference in the lives of many people!

Saying "thank you" is certainly wonderful, but let's make sure we embrace the thought and the feeling. Make it genuine and be sure to connect with the person you are thankful for. As Dale Carnegie said, "Flattery is from the teeth out. Sincere appreciation is from the heart out." You have developed your habit of gratitude into an attitude of gratitude, so now it's time to thank everybody for everything! Create your own holiday every day and watch others light up as they unwrap your gift of appreciation.

On an even deeper and more profound level, you may want to remember someone particularly special to you. No doubt there have been people in your life who have helped or inspired you in a meaningful way. Maybe it is someone you haven't seen or talked with in years—a school teacher or coach, a relative who lives across the country or a friend from college who got married and had children. Maybe it's someone you see every day but to whom you haven't given a well-deserved "thank you" in a long time. When Peggy was in high school she worked part-time in the registrar's office. Now, this lady had a tough reputation—none of the kids liked her and most people were afraid of her. However, what Peggy found was that she simply wanted (and needed) a friend—someone who appreciated how hard she worked and the contribution she made to the school. She had a daunting job—maintaining the records for hundreds of students. Peggy noticed the need and showed her appreciation. Peggy and this lady developed a life-long friendship that endured until her death more than 25 years after Peggy's graduation. They maintained their relationship through calls, occasional visits and holiday cards. She truly made an impact in Peggy's life.

If you'd like to recognize someone special in your life with an exceptional gift, we invite you to do the following exercise.

EXERCISE NINE: Write a letter of gratitude. Think of someone who has contributed to your well-being or growth—someone you feel you have never really thanked. Most people will think of a parent or other adult mentor in their life, but it can be anyone... a teacher, a friend, a business colleague, a customer or the nurse who watched over a loved one in the hospital. Write a letter to that person describing the benefits that person bestowed upon you. Don't type it. Don't email it. Write it in your own handwriting. Be detailed in your description of their actions and how their actions made you feel. Then deliver the letter in person. Read it aloud to that person and take enough time to be together to share your feelings. P.S. Do not—we repeat, do not—do this without a box of tissues!

It is good to be connected with others. Feeling and expressing gratitude to those who provide us with gifts will keep us connected by invisible threads of positive energy.

൝

*At times our own light goes out
and is rekindled by a spark
from another person.
Each of us has cause to think
with deep gratitude
of those who have lighted
the flame within us.*

— ALBERT SCHWEITZER

Gratitude expressions by Debbie

The two people for whom I am most grateful are the two people I have known the longest—my mother, who is presently 75 years old, and my father, who, sadly, died in 1998 when he was just

69 years old. Before I tell you about my wonderful parents, I want to share with you that I believe that nobody's life is perfect. How many times have you heard that before, yet you find yourself looking around, seeing people who seem happy and content and think that their life must be perfect? Appearances can be deceiving. A few months ago, in a lovely upscale neighborhood close to our home in Florida, a man shot and killed his wife and two young children and then he killed himself. Everybody in that community was shocked. Everything had seemed perfect for that family. They were loving and happy and well-liked by their neighbors and friends. Nobody suspected the troubles they had or thought they had.

That is an extreme example with an unusually tragic ending. I'm not suggesting that every family that seems loving and happy is not. Far from it. There are huge numbers of happy and loving families. What I am suggesting is that regardless of what your eyes tell you, everyone experiences some sadness in their life at some time. Loved ones die, we make bad financial decisions, someone steals from us, siblings fight and children get into trouble. We lose jobs, get into car accidents, get divorced and get sick. It may sound morbidly odd, but we need to recognize that bad things happen to other people just like they happen to us, not because we want to revel in another's misery, but because it is important to recognize and know we are not alone in our struggles. Remember the orientation exercise for the freshmen at college?

It is enormously important to realize that it is not just us who stumble or sometimes feel sad or overwhelmed. None of us is the odd man out—the one left behind on a sinking ship. Again, I do not say this because I think we should commiserate about each other's problems. I say this to point out that while you will see that I am grateful for my parents and other family members, know also that we have had our own struggles, and we still do! The question is what do you take away from your situation? You can have your struggles, and you can have gratitude, too!

My family never had a lot of extra money. My mother could stretch a dollar like nobody I know. Still can! More important to me, however, was that my mother always, always, always believed in me and supported the decisions I made. I'm not always a traditionalist. In fact, I do sometimes see myself as "the odd man out." When I decided to skip my senior year of high school and begin college early, my mother had doubts and second thoughts and even third thoughts, but ultimately she trusted my instincts and let me do it. It turned out to be one of the best decisions I ever made. Thanks, Mom! I was just 17 years old and my mother had the power to stop me, but I am grateful she knew it was okay to let me go.

When I decided to go to law school at age 33, my mother did not utter one negative word about my decision, although she did ask me the valid question "how will you afford it?" Neither of my parents could really afford the huge tuition and living expense associated with three more years of school and certainly it wasn't their obligation, either. And although I had worked for many years for the same law firm as a paralegal, I had not saved a lot of money. I actually don't remember the answer I gave my mother, because quite frankly I didn't have a plan, but we never spoke of it again and not because my mother didn't care. My mother has a bottomless well of love for both her daughters. Rather, my mother trusted that I would find a way to pay for law school, because she knew I really wanted to go and she had faith that I could accomplish anything I set my sights on. Three years later, I graduated from law school. I was fortunate that my father gave me some financial assistance, but that's the next story. As for my mother, she continues to this day to find ways to help me, and she has never tried to discourage me from anything I really wanted to do. She believed in me, and she still does. For that, I am immensely grateful, because the end result was that I grew fearless of challenge and change and now I see life as one adventure after another!

Not unlike other people, I had issues with my father growing up. I was around 10 years old when my parents separated. While they were separated, I discovered that my father loved my sister more than me. No, I have not invited you to a pity party! I don't remember being tremendously affected by my father's unequal feelings, but since it is such a strong memory, I assume it must have bothered me some. My parents reunited when I was about 12, and as I grew up, when I did something wrong, no matter how minor, my father's mantra would be "Can't you do anything right?" My father was also very, very tight with his money. Just ask my mother! It was hard to get even a few dollars out of him for a cheap pair of sunglasses. Although, again, we never had a lot of extra money, his thoughts about money were not based on lack of money, just a desire not to part with it! I simply learned to not ask my father for anything.

It might surprise you to learn that I loved my father very much all my life. We enjoyed a close relationship, and not just because he was my father and I had a duty to love him. Rather, I think that my father and I kind of grew up together. When I went back to college to get my Bachelor's degree (I had gotten an Associates in Science Degree when I was 18), I was 23 and didn't expect to receive financial assistance from my parents. One day a check arrived from my father. That continued for the two years I had left before receiving my degree, each check arriving at the precise moment I needed it. How did he know that? I never asked him for money—remember, I didn't ask my father for money anymore. Can you imagine how I felt when those checks arrived?! When I went to law school, after the first semester, my father also started sending me $500 a month until I graduated, money I never asked for but definitely appreciated.

What my father did for me while I was in college and in law school was one of the most amazing and special things that he ever could have done for me. It wasn't just about the money. I was, of course, exceedingly grateful for the financial help. However, what was most significant to me was that my father, who hated parting with his money, was making a gift to me because he saw a need and wanted to help! And, knowing how my father felt about money, I knew this was a real sacrifice for him.

At some point my father also had stopped saying "can't you do anything right" and eventually I felt he loved me and my sister equally—that my father loved me as much as any father loved his daughter. Shortly after I graduated from college—I still remember the moment—I had a profound revelation—that my father had not been born with a parenting book in his hand. Ok, not a novel inspiration but one that helped me see my father as a growing, loving human being. I loved my father for the person he was and grew to be and for the person he helped me become. I am grateful that my father was my father, that he was who he was, for everything he taught me and for the times we could be honest with each other. Some may see bad times in my story, but I see learning times.

There are so many others I am grateful for, like my sister and her family, my friends, and those in the cruising community. However, I will add one more significant note, this one about Craig, my terrific husband of 10 years. Craig has opened my world and from him I have learned patience, tolerance and the value of good communication, among other things. I am also grateful not only that Craig is interested in my personal growth but his own as well. I love hugs, so I'm really grateful when Craig says "I haven't gotten my hug today." I think he says that just so I think he loves hugs as much as I do, but that's okay—I'll take a hug from him any way I can get it. My list could go on, but mostly, I am grateful that I get to spend the rest of my life with this man!

Gratitude expressions by Peggy

I am grateful every day for all of my blessings—my husband, pets, family, friends, business opportunities—everything. So, it's hard to pick a single example. I could, of course, appreciate my grandparents, my parents or my husband—and I'm tempted. But, for today, I'm going to appreciate two of my horses, Reno and Tahoe.

Reno and Tahoe are wild mustangs, born in the hills of Nevada. They were destined to be free, but man changed all of that. Specifically, the Bureau of Land Management (BLM), an agency of our government. Between the ranchers and the BLM, there doesn't seem to be enough property to house both wild horses and cattle. Unfortunately, the "solution" to this problem is to remove the horses from government lands, and then attempt to re-adopt them into private homes. The unlucky ones will likely end up at the slaughterhouse.

I imagine for the first few months of their lives, Reno and Tahoe had few worries. They lived by their instincts, bred into them through hundreds of generations of collective conscience. They followed the lead of the mares and the stallion that protected the herd. They were young, strong and had every reason to believe they would live free, forever.

Then one day, probably without much warning, man appeared on the scene with a goal—to capture the mustangs. They, along with many others, were rounded up and placed in a holding pen. I can only imagine the terror they felt—nothing was as it should be. I'm sure there was confusion and chaos. Were they separated from their mothers then, or did that come later? In any event, they were eventually separated from the only security they had known—their mothers and the safety of the wild herd. Now they were prisoners, captives who would be required to eat what was provided, share space with other captives and go where they were urged.

Ultimately they ended up at an adoption facility in Ocala, Florida. Several weeks earlier, I had made the decision to adopt a horse or two for me and my husband, Joe. We had recently moved to five acres in the country. I had initially promised I would wait a year or so before bringing home any horses. That promise was short-lived. Less than six months later, I announced my decision to become a horse owner. I had owned horses as a child, but this would be my first experience as a horse owner as an adult where I would have the sole responsibility—physically, emotionally and financially—for the care of my horses. I loved the sound of it—my horses.

The challenge was to find the perfect horse. Growing up I had been blessed with two horses. The first was an unruly two-year-old Arab-Welsh cross named Mint Julep. She and I were both young and inexperienced. It didn't stop either one of us. Soon we were seen everywhere together—never mind the weather. We walked, trotted, cantered, galloped and jumped our way around the Maryland country side. My second horse, Vain Ruler (called Lady for short) was a Thoroughbred off the racetrack. I even saw her run in her last race! She was really something the day she arrived—all shiny, muscular and terrified. From that day forward she never allowed another man to touch her. We ultimately made our peace and she became my mount (albeit somewhat unreliable). But she could run like the wind! The point of telling you about Julep and Lady is that I had my early challenges with horses. I like to say I never had a trained horse. I now had the chance to change my track record (no pun intended).

Instead, a friend gave me a "great" idea. I should adopt two wild mustangs from the upcoming BLM adoption. Mustangs—real wild horses! This was a young girl's dream come true. I was fascinated with the idea of a wild horse—I even had one of the actual photographs from the Congressional hearings when they passed the Wild Horse and Burro Act in the 1970's. I had met Wild Horse Annie. I had sponsored a young mustang on a preserve. I gave presentations at school and at 4-H on mustangs. The idea that I would ever actually own one had never crossed my mind. Once this idea took hold, I could think of nothing else. I located the appropriate applications so I could be approved as a "foster" home for the mustangs I intended to adopt. The BLM actually has an approval process and minimum requirements for the transportation and maintenance of the horses. After adoption, I would have only conditional ownership for a year where I would have to then prove my horses were in good health and had not been sold to a slaughterhouse or otherwise abused.

I had several panic attacks in the weeks leading up to the adoption. I couldn't believe I was actually going to adopt a wild mustang—and two of them at that! What was I thinking? They were just weanlings—barely away from their mothers. It would be years before they could be ridden. These horses were far from my original idea of finding the "perfect horse."

The day of the adoption arrived. My friend Lisa and I travelled with her horse trailer to Ocala. We arrived early to get a good look at the horses that would be available that day. Upon entering the facility, I nearly had a heart attack. I don't know what I expected, but this wasn't it. This was the most mangy, straggly, unkempt bunch of horses I had ever seen. And there were more than a hundred of them! How would I ever find my perfect horse? My husband had admonished me to "pick a big one" for him. I didn't even know what I wanted for myself. There were palominos, buckskins, chestnuts, blacks, bays, cremellos—every color of the horse rainbow. My head was spinning. There were too many. You couldn't tell one from the other and they kept moving around. The only form of identification they had was a tag around their necks. I was writing fast and furious, trying to keep them all straight. Which were to be mine? Fate would have to decide—and she did.

Ultimately, Reno and Tahoe were selected, corralled, paid for and then transported home. Upon reaching the house—I think I held my breath the whole way—my husband eagerly awaited my new prized possessions. When they were released (I hesitate to say unloaded—because that would imply we had had some say in the matter), he gasped! They were small, scrawny and looked like yaks. They were matted and dirty, with long ratty manes the cowboys had chopped in places with a knife. Their thick Nevada coats looked like a dirty moth-eaten sweater. I was smiling ear to ear!

Now the lessons would begin—mine and theirs—mostly mine. It was several weeks before they could be approached and touched. Don't forget, these are wild horses, born to be wild, never to be touched or loved by a human. They had been traumatized and they were not going to have anything to do with anyone sporting two legs.

I have never been a patient person. I still have an impatient streak, but I am worlds better—because of Reno and Tahoe. I was smart enough to hire a trainer—someone with wild horse experience. For years we diligently worked with Reno and Tahoe. First, to gentle them to our presence and our touch. Then, to allow us to brush them and pick up their feet. Next, to allow them to be led where we wanted them to go (instead of vice versa). Every day, we learned something new and the bond between us deepened. Soon they were working in the round pen—trotting and cantering circles around me on an invisible cord. They would change their speed, turn, stop, come to me—all with the use of body language and the tone of my voice. Eventually, the day came when I decided it was time to get on Tahoe's back. I was there just a few moments before all hell broke loose! He bucked—hard. I flew up in the air, nearly did a flip and landed on the ground. Joe, who was "holding" my horse, burned his hands with the lead rope. Gratefully, no one was seriously injured.

Soon, both Reno and Tahoe were under saddle and the lessons continued. I fell off. I got back on. I fell off again. I got back on. They spooked, I fell off. I got back on. This went on for what seemed like years. I was wishing their lives away. First I wanted them to be two so I could ride them. Then I wanted them to be five so they would have some experience and I wouldn't have to keep falling off. Then I wanted them to be seven because that's when everyone says a horse gets smart (and good). My horses obviously didn't read the same books I did. They continued to challenge my authority as their leader and role model.

I have hundreds of memories of my time with them, which are embedded in my soul forever. Today, my wild mustangs are thirteen years old and still a challenge. The challenges have changed over the years. Now they are more like big dogs than wild horses. They come when they are called, are easily handled and can be ridden (usually without fear). Reno turned out to be smart—like a fox. He has managed to avoid anyone riding him for a couple of years now. He made the experience so unpleasant that we just gave up. Not that he was mean or scary—instead, lazy, ornery, clumsy and seemingly stupid." Tahoe, on the other hand, can still be scary but he's mostly a lot of fun. He has never lost his instinct that tells him, "run like hell and ask questions later." Today, he suffers from a nervous system disorder that causes him to have epileptic seizures. The medical community cannot tell me the cause or the cure, only that he requires daily medication. Some may have taken another route—not me—he's my heart.

Reno and Tahoe have been one of the great experiences of my lifetime. My heart soars when I look out the window and see them lazily grazing in the back pasture. With me, they have a forever home. My husband likes to refer to them as the "freeloaders" but they've paid their debt. They gave up their freedom, not by choice, but by destiny. They have blessed me in innumerable ways. They have changed me forever—helped me become the person I am today and the one I want to be tomorrow. And the lessons keep on coming.

A Gratitude Campaign

Scott Truitt started a profound and significant gratitude campaign that we think everyone will want to join, especially those of us who sometimes feel awkward expressing our gratitude. Scott wanted a way to easily and comfortably say thanks to the military and other service personnel we all pass in airports, shopping centers and on the street. As Scott put it, "Whether you believe in the reasons for going over there or not, you still have to support our AMERICAN troops that are there."

We urge you to check out and join Scott's effort to spread the recognition and appreciation we so often feel for our military and other service personnel but just don't know how to express. Learn more about Scott's vision and how you can easily join his campaign at *GratitudeCampaign.org.* There you will have the opportunity to watch an amazing and heartfelt video about using American Sign Language to convey your thanks! As Scott says, "It's not about politics. It's about service, and sacrifice, and it's about gratitude... give them a sign."

Your Gratitude Expressions

We recommend you record your expressions of gratitude daily. We hope our five-year *Gratitude Expressions* journal will help you accomplish that goal. The important thing is to be grateful, show appreciation, and record your thoughts surrounding your feelings. It will set the tone for your day and your life. ❧

You have it easily in your power
to increase the sum total
of this world's happiness now. How?
By giving a few words
of sincere appreciation to someone
who is lonely or discouraged.
Perhaps you will forget tomorrow
the kind words you say today,
But the recipient may cherish
them over a lifetime.

—DALE CARNEGIE

CHAPTER 8

❦

Making a Living Through Giving

*Pretend that every single person
you meet has a sign
around his or her neck that says,
Make Me Feel Important.
Not only will you succeed in sales,
you will succeed in life.*

—MARY KAY ASH

So far we've talked a lot about gratitude and its importance in your daily living. Can gratitude be of any value in your business life as well? Kody Bateman, founder and CEO of SendOutCards encourages people to "make a living through giving." As we have been discussing in this book, Kody is an advocate for feeling and showing genuine appreciation and watching the benefits that naturally flow from that emotion. You can make a great living when you make appreciation and gratitude an important part of your business. Unfortunately, lots of people think that in order to be successful, you can't be kind.

In a conversation just the other day, someone expressed their belief that to be truly successful, you have to have a ruthless "it's all about me" side to you. We hope that's not true. In fact, Kody has proved it's not true. He and increasing numbers of individuals inside his organization are discovering you can be successful if you stay focused on what's really important—counting your blessings every day and showing sincere gratitude and appreciation for all the people in both your personal life and your business life.

The SendOutCards organization was created to assist people in acting on their "promptings." As described by Kody Bateman, "a prompting is a feeling, nudge, a fleeting thought or an inner voice that gives each of us personal insight." A prompting should be our clue to acknowledge or recognize someone in our life. That recognition can come in many forms, such as a phone call, a hug, a thoughtful gesture, a gift or a card. As long as you are responding to the prompting by taking positive action, you've accomplished your goal. The easier it is to act on a prompting, the more likely you are to take that positive step. If it's difficult, expensive or can be easily forgotten, the likelihood is you won't take that positive step and you may ultimately regret the outcome. This is what happened in Kody's life.

In 1989, Kody was moving across country with his young wife and daughter to their new home in New York City. On their way out of town, they went by Kody's parents' home to say good-bye. As Kody went to leave and get in his car, he saw his brother, Kris, moving some cars around. At that time, he had a very strong prompting that he should to walk over and hug his brother to say goodbye. It was unusual for his family to hug and Kody was in a hurry, so he ignored this prompting and instead simply got into his car, honked and waved goodbye to his brother. Two months later, Kody received a telephone call from his mother telling him that his brother Kris had been killed in an accident. Kody realized he had missed an opportunity to show and tell his brother how much he loved him. As a result, Kody made a promise to himself and his brother that he would never again fail to act on his promptings and he would develop a way for others to easily act on their promptings.

We sometimes make a written note to ourselves about the promptings we have. It may be a notation to send a card to congratulate a friend for something wonderful or to encourage a client facing an upcoming surgery. It might be a note to make a phone call to say "hi" to someone we haven't seen or talked with in a while. Or it might be a note reminding us to acknowledge a birthday, anniversary or special occasion. Our promptings evidence the connections we have to the people we care about. How many times have you had the experience of thinking about someone and when you call them, they say they were just thinking about you? We believe this happens often and it happens because of promptings and the energy that keeps us connected throughout the universe.

Promptings represent your inner guide telling you how to behave so you can make a difference in another person's (or your own) life. Promptings should not be ignored or put on the back burner—they should be acted on immediately (or as close as possible to the time you received the prompting). They should never be forgotten.

We mentioned that some people will make a note when they have a prompting. While most people probably make notes about birthdays, anniversaries, holidays and the like, we think most people do not make notes about the more unusual promptings. Most people probably do not make a written note when prompted to reach out to someone for such things as congratulations on a new job or new house, sympathy for the loss of a loved one or a beloved pet, or just to say "hi" because they were thinking of someone. For those people who do not make a written note, the mental note is gone and usually forgotten if not acted upon literally in minutes. The opportunity to connect with somebody you were called to think of and reach out to evaporates quickly, and the person you were thinking of may never know of your joy or concern for their circumstances—they may never know that you thought of them in a kind and caring way at that moment. Wouldn't it be special if they did?

Discover for yourself how best to respond to your promptings. Be aware of how, when and where they show up. How are you going to make sure you always act on those promptings? How are you going to make sure the special people in your life always know when you are thinking of them?

Adopt gratitude and appreciation as a business model

Gratitude and appreciation are unquestionably an important part of our personal lives. Gratitude and appreciation can, and should also form the core of your business model. You will stand out from your competitors if you *feel and express* genuine appreciation for your current and potential customers, clients and referral sources. We are constantly amazed how few people are genuinely appreciative of their customers or clients.

Peggy travels frequently and likes to stay in family owned and operated bed and breakfast establishments. In the many years she has been doing this, only once has she received an expression of appreciation for her patronage. Yet it seems logical that if the business owner wanted to encourage Peggy and her family to return, they would take a positive form of action—some sign of gratitude—to let her know they appreciated her business (or her referrals). How difficult and/or expensive would it be for these establishments to send a heartfelt thank you and maybe even a certificate for a discount on a future stay?

If you are in business, how do you show appreciation for your current and potential customers or clients and referral sources? When you complete a big sale or transaction, do you send a note or gift to say a warm thank you? Do you send a regular newsletter keeping them informed of relevant facts related to their concerns? Do you send a birthday, anniversary or holiday greeting card to let them know they are remembered and appreciated? If you do send end-of-year holiday greeting cards but no cards during the rest of the year, why not?! Do you want your customers or clients to remember you only at the end of the year, or would you like them to remember you in July and on their birthday? If you want them to remember you throughout the year, you must show that you remember them throughout the year.

Do you go the extra mile by holding annual (or more frequent) client appreciation events and then sending your clients a note or card thanking them for coming? Do you ever call to say you are just simply thinking about that individual? What you do to appreciate the people who provide you with a living says a lot about your character, especially to those you work with—and perhaps will be an indication of your future success. Maya Angelou said "People will forget what you said, they will forget what you did, but they will never forget how you make them feel." Take a moment to think about this. How do you make people feel?

Peggy recently had minor surgery. A day or so after the surgery, the doctor's office called to inquire how she was feeling and if she had any questions, comments or concerns about the recent procedure. It showed genuine concern for her well-being on the part of that office.

When Peggy bought a car a year or so ago, the salesperson followed up with a series of thank you notes and a box of cookies! These small gestures made Peggy feel like the money she spent at that business and with that sales person was really appreciated. Next time she buys a car, do you think she'll give that person or dealership another try? The answer is—it depends.

If Peggy doesn't buy another car for a couple of years, what is the likelihood the same salesperson is still going to be employed there? Is she going to remember his name if he hasn't made an effort since the initial sale to stay in touch? If he's left the business, has he advised his customers where he's gone and invited them to visit at this new location? What is the dealership doing to capitalize on the goodwill generated by his earlier activities? The likelihood is, they may do nothing to maintain the original goodwill generated by the earlier activities. If they don't stay in touch, they will soon be forgotten!

Peggy's dad bought cars from the same salesman for more than 30 years. Now this guy did a great job. He so endeared himself to the Hoyt family that he attended family events and became a genuine friend. It didn't matter where he was employed, John Hoyt was going to buy a car from Cy Gatewood. Notice that Peggy still remembers him well, as several of her cars were also purchased from him.

Unfortunately, Debbie and her husband had the opposite experience recently. They just returned from cruising on their boat for two years and needed a second car. They are thorough shoppers and, as a result, have visited many dealerships. Debbie has given her card or their names to multiple salespeople. A few months ago, they specifically asked one salesman to call them in a few months to let them know vehicle availability, as they were not quite ready to purchase. He never called. In fact, only one—out of probably 7 or 8—salespeople called to follow up with Debbie and her husband. We find that astounding! There is no question the Rosers are going to buy a car… someone is going to make a commission… but only one salesperson understands the concept of developing relationships to grow the business. Debbie and Craig have repeatedly been sent the message that their business is not important.

Most people cannot tell you the name of the person they bought their home from if more than a year has elapsed since that purchase. How sad for the realtors—they could have been building continued goodwill and a great source of future referrals if they had genuinely appreciated the customer for the initial sale and then taken the extra steps to keep their name at the top of that customer's mind. Top of mind awareness can be critical to the success of your business—we take for granted that the people we've done business with are going to remember us. Were we really that memorable? The first important question is "how did you make them feel?" The second and perhaps more important question is, "how do you continue to make them feel?" The passage of time has a funny way of dimming people's memories—they need active and regular appreciation reminders to keep the idea of doing business with you fresh in their mind.

How can you continue to remind the people you do business with of your value-added proposition? We suggest the development of an appreciation model of doing business.

EXERCISE TEN: List everything you do to show appreciation to your current or potential clients or customers and referral sources. What else can you do? How often do they hear from you? How often do they hear from you without you trying to sell them something? How often do they hear simply that you are thinking of them? How many would recognize your name and welcome your call if you picked up the phone and called? How many would expect that you were just calling to talk business, sell or collect a fee? How many of your current or potential clients or customers and referral sources have you called this week simply to say hello?

Think of all the ways you have been appreciated in the past by people you have done business with who you remember and value. How did it make you feel? Do you think it's important that you make your customers or clients feel that way? Can that form of appreciation be adapted to your business? What else might you do that is different and would set you apart from your competitors? What is your business value proposition and how can you use it to uniquely appreciate each one of your clients on a regular and ongoing basis?

Peggy works with financial advisors as part of her legal practice. Many of them work for the same company so her practice may get multiple e-newsletters that are all exactly the same. How can you differentiate yourself? Is your newsletter coming by email or snail mail? Is your picture on the front so your face, as well as your name, stays fresh?

There are an unlimited assortment of gimmicks in the world. You can try those if you like, but we recommend gratitude and appreciation for the customers who have enriched your business with their patronage and loyalty, and that it be genuine! Your customers will see through not only the gimmicks but also disingenuous gratitude. For genuine gratitude, you don't have to spend a lot of money, but you do need to invest some time and energy to create an appreciation model that works for you and your business.

We do business not only with people we like, but people we can remember. Your customers will remember you if you remember them. It's all about connections. You know you need to stay connected to family and friends in order to maintain those relationships. It's exactly the same with your customers—you must stay connected!

Your customers will remember you best if their experience is unique and genuine and when they feel you truly care about them as people and the experience they had as part of your service. The Disney organization is one of the best at this—they have created memorable experiences that people simply do not forget. What are people remembering about their experience with you or your company?

Customers don't spend money as a favor to us—they do it in exchange for something of value. What they perceive as value may be different from your perception, but the fact remains that if they perceive a high value, they'll pay more and they are more likely to come back for more. If they perceive a low value, they'll expect to pay less (or in some cases, nothing at all) and the likelihood they will return is small. How can you help increase their perception of value? Remembering them in ways that communicate your appreciation of them and their business is one significant way.

Have you ever patronized a business and didn't get what you bargained for? I'm sure you have—we all have. How did that business handle your complaint? Or did you remain silent—not even letting them know they disappointed you? Did you offer a suggestion for how they might improve their service in your area of disappointment? Did they offer to do anything to compensate you for your dissatisfaction? Did they apologize? What could they have done to make the situation better and repair the damage to their reputation?

Years ago, Peggy and her husband, Joe determined they were no longer going to tolerate bad or unacceptable service. If they received a level of service that did not meet their expectations, they vowed to inform the business owner and ask for reparations. As a result, there have been some pretty interesting responses. Peggy prides herself on her letter writing ability—letters that get attention. A letter to the president of a retail boot and clothing store resulted in an obviously hand-typed letter of apology as well as a gift certificate to "bribe" her back into the store. A letter to the president of a well-known overnight delivery company resulted in a series of letters back and forth with a customer service representative and was ultimately resolved with a significant gift certificate. It didn't completely remove the negative effects of their bad service, but it sure did help. Not only should you acknowledge your customer and their complaint but also resolve it to their satisfaction. Then, consider following up with a "thank you for letting us correct the problem" note. All of that goes a long way to rebuilding your reputation and turning your potentially former customers into loyal customers.

Peggy recently complained to the president of a well-known jewelry chain about a series of negative experiences. The store's response was to have the manager call—but there was no response from the president—the person to whom the letter was written. Peggy no longer intends to do business with that establishment. A simple response from the right person may have been sufficient to retain a long-time loyal customer. Interestingly, there is one person employed by this jewelry chain who has made it her business to go above and beyond for her clients and she is the only bright side to an otherwise disappointing experience.

Debbie recently had a similar experience with her insurance agent. The agent has one employee who has single-handedly made the Rosers feel welcome to that agency. She consistently goes the extra mile not only to take care of the Rosers but also to communicate with them, making them feel a part of the agency family. Unfortunately, telephone calls recently made directly to the agent herself by both Debbie and Craig, on different matters, were repeatedly ignored. The agent never returned their calls. Is it any wonder why the Rosers are considering taking their business to another agency?!

The accessibility of the Internet has changed the way we do business. We no longer have just a local or national economy but a global one. Products have become commoditized, resulting in price pressures for producers. Think about where and how you bought the most recent items you purchased. Did you get in your car, drive all over town and ultimately find the thing you were seeking? Or did you start with the Internet to do your research, ultimately discovering the best value proposition for your needs and then either going directly to that provider or purchasing the item on line? What about service businesses—doctors, lawyers, plumbers, carpet cleaners? It's a little harder to purchase those services on line but we still might do our research there to discover if they are well-represented and highly regarded. Today, it's almost impossible not to have an Internet presence—just for that reason. As the social media sites become more popular, businesses are being forced to stay technologically alert just to keep pace with the trends.

Do you have a way of communicating your value proposition to your clients that puts you in the best possible light? Are you generating business leads using social media? If so, how do you communicate with those people to show them what you can do and how you will appreciate their business in the future? We've both signed up for many Internet based newsletters and information. The Internet is an unlimited source of information—in fact, more than you really need. The challenge is distilling the noise from the true, accurate information. As a result, your message should be short, succinct and reflect your unique value proposition. It should not (in our opinion) always be a solicitation for more business.

Peggy recently signed up for a great on-line video regarding social media services. She really enjoyed it and learned a great deal—even sharing the site with others. However, since then she has received hundreds of emails from the producer with endless solicitations for purchasing more and more products. Yuk! It is a total turn off and the ultimate result was a request to unsubscribe from future mailings. We also think it is difficult to develop a real relationship with someone solely through the use of email and social media networking sites. Again, people are just sick of culling through tens or hundreds of emails each day. You must have a more tangible way of reaching out to people. Ultimately, the Internet can become a pest—one you want to smash just to get rid of it.

You only hear from some businesses when they want something from you. It's time for your next appointment or they are trying to up sell you on a product you already own. From these businesses, you will only get communication related to what they

Making a Living Through Giving

want or need—never to acknowledge or appreciate you or your patronage. If this has been your business model, seek out ways to touch your clients that are not related to a request for more business, but instead represents a genuine appreciation for the business they have given you in the past.

Make it personal

Today, only about 3% of the mail we receive is personal. Do you remember when it was fun to go to the mailbox, because there might be a letter, note or card from someone? Now, we dread it because we're pretty sure all we'll find are bills and junk.

If you are our age—and we're not disclosing—you will remember when writing letters by hand and sending them by snail mail was the norm. We actually used to write letters! When Debbie was in law school, she corresponded regularly—more than once a month—with her father. What a treat it was to go to the mailbox and see a letter from her dad. She didn't even have to know what he said to be thrilled that he had thought of her and had taken the time to let her know! Growing up, Debbie used to write often to her great aunt. Once she decided to type her letter so she could write more, and more efficiently. In response, her aunt sent her a box of fancy writing paper! It was a subtle but profound message. Her aunt wanted the personal touch of a hand written note. Debbie never sent her aunt another typewritten letter, and if her aunt was alive today, she certainly wouldn't send her email!

Seriously, email serves a wonderful purpose, both in our personal and business lives. It allows us instant communication for quick catch-up notes. We find, however, that most people, when they talk about email, usually say something like "I was gone for a few days and now I have 436 email messages, ugh!" If any of those are jokes or e-cards, it is likely they will not get much, if any, notice and will probably get a quick stab of the "delete" key. Seriously, how much of your email is personal?! We have come to dread email as much as snail mail, because there is just so much of it and it has come to consume more of our time than we would like. For those who are frazzled or otherwise associate email with negative connotations, those negative feelings will carry over to the well-meaning jokes and e-cards that were sent to try to lighten one's day. Jokes and e-cards may totally miss their mark when the recipient has limited time to get through just the emails that are relevant or important to family or business issues. The fact remains, the feeling one gets from getting an email doesn't even come close to the feeling one gets from receiving a personal heartfelt card or note in ye old snail mail.

When was the last time you received a personal card in your mailbox? Can you remember how it made you feel? Wouldn't you love it if more people sent you real cards in the mail more often? When was the last time you sent a real card, either to a friend or family member or even to a customer? People today don't send many cards anymore. It is inconvenient, time consuming and expensive and often we simply forget because we didn't act on the prompting soon enough.

When it comes to your business, sending a card to your current or potential customers or clients and referral sources can give you a tremendous advantage over your competitors. When you remember your customers throughout the year, they will remember you throughout the year! Think about it. If you were to send out 5 cards throughout the year to each customer just to let them know that you are thinking about them and appreciate their business, how would that make them feel? Then, when that customer or someone they know needs the product or service you offer, do you think they will think of you? You were the person who cared enough to take the time to think of them—not your competitor down the street who sends out nothing or only correspondence to promote his product or service.

You may not realize it, but most people care less about what you have to sell them than what you think about them and how you make them feel. Sending a note or a card can be an easy, convenient and inexpensive way to build and maintain relationships in your business. When you have a relationship with your customers, they generally won't leave you, but like any good relationship, it takes effort. What if you never showed appreciation to your spouse ever again? How long do you think you could sustain that relationship? It's no different in business. Providing the best price is not a reliable relationship builder. What your customers want is a good product, good service, good value *and* to be noticed and appreciated. As a business owner, an important part of your job is to communicate to your customers that they are important to you. A heartfelt note or card is an excellent way to accomplish that goal.

SendOutCards

As we mentioned, however, sending out cards can be inconvenient, time consuming and expensive. We know we should do it, but it seems like such an onerous task, especially if you have hundreds of current and potential customers or clients and referral sources. Even sending out 10 cards a month can be daunting. Kody Bateman did us a wonderful service when he created SendOutCards.

SendOutCards is an online greeting card creation company. If you have access to the internet, you can create and send a greeting card in about a minute, for about $1.00, including postage, without leaving your home or office! You create the card, click the "send" button, and your card is printed, stuffed, stamped and put in the mail for you. You also have the option of uploading photographs to the front and/or inside of the card for that extra "wow factor" and staying power. You can even include a gift or gift card, Plus, you can choose to write the card in your own handwriting and sign it with your own signature. Anywhere you have access to the Internet, you can send a real card!

Debbie and her husband recently spent a few months in the Bahamas on their sailboat. They were in the more remote areas when Debbie received an email from a good friend from college informing her that her father had passed away quite suddenly. Here's what Debbie writes about that:

> I was terribly saddened by the news. My friend's parents practically adopted me when we were in college, and my

friend was very, very close to her dad. I wanted to send condolence cards to my friend and her mother and her daughter. There was no way I was just going to send an email! So I went to land in search of cards. I quickly learned that finding a card in the more remote areas of the Bahamas (which is most of the Bahamas) was going to be near impossible. Luckily I at least had the foresight to pack blank note cards. It was not the ideal for me, but I wrote my notes and took them ashore. Well, it was several days before I could find an open post office so I could attach the correct postage and mail the notes. This was getting frustrating! If that wasn't enough, those cards took about three weeks to arrive. Most of the areas in the Bahamas are serviced by mail boats that arrive only once a week, and then those mail boats go to Nassau to unload. I only wish I had known about SendOutCards when this was happening. I could have chosen the card I wanted, written what I wanted to say, and sent those cards off within a matter of minutes of receiving my friend's email.

We would agree that the fact that Debbie was not able to get cards to her friend and her friend's family right away was not the end of the world. However, when we think of someone and want to acknowledge them and what they may be going through, whether happy or sad, it is important to us that we can do it when we want to do it. SendOutCards totally solves that problem. What if you receive a prompting when you are on a business trip, especially in a foreign country where it is likely the cards you do find will be in a foreign language? Are you going to be comfortable ignoring that prompting or would you be thrilled to be able to act on that prompting?

What if you want to send out lots of cards? It may sound easy to send a card to one person, but what if you want to send a card to one hundred or more people in recognition of Independence Day or St. Patrick's Day or the Christmas holiday? No problem. It's just as easy, convenient and quick with the SendOutCards system to send a card to one person as it is to send a card to many people. After you create your card, you choose the recipients by going into your contact manager and checking a box next to the name of each person you want to receive the card. Then, as before, you simply click "send," and off the card will go to each and every person checked. Whether you want to send a card to one person, 100 people or 500 people, you can still do it in about a minute—not each card but total time. And you can do it for as little as about $1.00 per card. For a small investment of time, many people will know you were thinking of them that day.

In the summer of 2009, Debbie took her 3-year-old great nephew, Elijah, for swim lessons, because her sister—his grandmother—had installed a pool and everyone thought it would be a good idea to get him acclimated to the water, even though there was a baby fence around the pool. The lessons took place during the day, when Elijah's parents were working. Since Elijah's parents couldn't come to watch the lessons, Debbie's Mom took pictures to record Elijah's first swim lessons. Then Debbie chose a few pictures and created a card with those pictures in and on the card.

She also designed the card to come from Elijah and addressed it to "Mommy and Daddy." Inside, Elijah told his parents how much fun he had and how much he learned. They absolutely loved it. That is one card that will never get thrown away!

Peggy regularly sends birthday and anniversary cards to her clients. And they regularly call her to thank her for the cards! Isn't that amazing? You send a card to someone for the sole reason of letting them know you are thinking of them, and they call to thank you! That's how it is when you show you care. Show your customers you care, and they will care about you and about doing business with you! ଔ

ଔ

*If you wish your merit
to be known,
acknowledge that of
other people.*

— ORIENTAL PROVERB

CHAPTER 9

Appreciation Marketing and Relationship Marketing

No one who achieves success does so without acknowledging the help of others. The wise and confident acknowledge this help with gratitude.

—AUTHOR UNKNOWN

You can grow both your life and business through appreciation. In business, when you value your customers and clients and share your appreciation with them, you gain return appreciation and loyalty. This is the cornerstone of the newly coined phrase "appreciation marketing."

Appreciation marketing focuses on true, genuine gratitude for past or future business, the goal being to give, not to get. Appreciation marketing is not sending out letters or flyers seeking new business from your customers. It's also not sending out letters or cards saying "Thanks, and, by the way, come on in and let me sell you…" It is the communication of a simple "thank you" for business.

There are a variety of ways to convey that simple "thank you," as we have shared in prior chapters. Whether you hold client appreciation events or send out letters, cards or gifts, it is just a matter of finding a way to communicate to customers and clients that you value their business.

EXERCISE ELEVEN: *Today thank a client/customer/referral source for their business. Do the same tomorrow and every day following.*

"Relationship marketing" is a bit different from appreciation marketing. A business that employs relationship marketing understands not only that customers and clients should be recognized and appreciated, but that it makes good sense and it is good business to develop relationships with those we serve. Those businesses focus not so much on a single transaction but on the development of a relationship. Remember Peggy's story about Cy Gatewood and her dad? Cy Gatewood sold Peggy's dad a car and then built a lasting friendship with her family. As Peggy wrote, "It didn't matter where he was employed, John Hoyt was going to buy a car from Cy Gatewood."

Relationship marketing recognizes the long term value of keeping customers and clients, as opposed to simply acquiring new clients. The concepts of appreciation marketing and relationship marketing are complementary. We want to attract and keep clients through relationship marketing and then support and nurture that relationship through genuine and heartfelt demonstrations of appreciation.

As lawyers, both Debbie and Peggy have built their businesses and reputations through the development of relationships. Peggy's practice is based on the philosophy "Partners in Planning, Friends for Life." That philosophy demonstrates a commitment to lifelong client relationships, not one that exists only long enough to collect the fee. It also means that Peggy and her partner only work with people they like, people with whom they truly want to be friends.

Have you ever had an experience with someone who led you to believe they wanted a relationship but as soon as the "transaction" was complete, that was the last time you ever saw or heard from that person? We both have, in many situations, and we were always disappointed. These were people who were out to "get" something—not to give something without the expectation of something in return. We all want to be paid for the services and products we provide—we are not saying that shouldn't be your ultimate goal. But, it can't and shouldn't be your *only* goal. How you get to that goal and how you treat your clients after reaching that goal will be the true reflection of your inner driving force.

Both relationship marketing and appreciation marketing are tools you can use to support your daily sales efforts and distinguish you from your competition. That should be a primary goal—to be so different from your competition that there really is no competition at all because no one is doing what you are doing or in the same way. This is what is referred to as a blue ocean strategy. The aim of the blue ocean strategy, as described by its creators, W. Chan Kim and Renée Mauborgne, "is not to out-perform the competition in the existing industry, but to create new market space or a blue ocean, thereby making the competition irrelevant." If the competition were irrelevant, business should be booming!

We are surprised when we talk to people about appreciation marketing and their response is, "I really don't have the time, energy, resources (et cetera), for appreciating and staying in touch with my clients." What you should be saying instead is that you don't have the time, energy, resources, et cetera, not to! If you don't invest in those appreciation activities that will endear you to your prospects and clients, you may find you will continuously work harder and harder with fewer and fewer rewards.

> You cannot do a kindness too soon because you never know how soon it will be too late.
> — RALPH WALDO EMERSON

Remember also that in business, it is not only the customers and clients who are necessary and important to our success. The individuals who work in our business and for our business are also worthy of appreciation. Sometimes we forget that the people we see every day in our business also crave appreciation in ways other than the paycheck. We get into a rut. We enter the door and focus on the task of producing results. Everyone regularly needs a pat on the back. Remember, one pat on the back will lead to another. Try this exercise and see if happiness spreads at your business today.

EXERCISE TWELVE: *Today thank someone at work for something you feel is simply part of their job. Do the same thing tomorrow and every day following. Watch for individual reactions and record your observations.*

Many businesses have regular team meetings. Mary Kay remains one of, if not the most successful woman entrepreneur of all time. In her book, *Miracles Happen,* she wrote about the company's sales meetings, traditionally held on Mondays. This is what Mary Kay wrote about those meetings:

> To many people, Monday signals the end of a carefree weekend and the beginning of a work week. But if the last week was not good for you, it was good for someone else! So we often tell our Consultants, "If you had a bad week, you need the unit meeting; if you had a good week, the unit meeting needs you!" When a Consultant leaves the inspiration, motivation, and enthusiasm of a Monday unit meeting, she has an entire week to let all that excitement work for her. The whole week starts off in high gear.

If you do not conduct regular team meetings, sales meetings or other meetings, consider starting them. They are a great way to maintain inspiration in your business. If you will start these meetings, or if you already conduct meetings, consider the words of Mary Kay and consider also making the next exercise a priority at every meeting.

EXERCISE THIRTEEN: *In your business, begin each regular team, sales and any other type of meeting with a positive round—what's going well. End each meeting with recognition and appreciation. You can do a round robin so everyone gets a turn.*

If you appreciate your team, your team will appreciate you. That appreciation will also be reflected in the way your team treats and cares for your prospects and clients. We are all part of the whole—no one exists independently and, we can't say it enough, everyone thrives on appreciation.

Peggy's law firm tries to do a few appreciation events each year. Some are designed for clients, others just for the team. Recently, the Hoyt & Bryan team celebrated a team member birthday at lunch and from there went to a chocolate factory where they spent the afternoon "making" and eating chocolate and enjoying everyone's company. The following Monday at the team meeting everyone commented during the appreciation round how much they enjoyed the time spent together away from the office as well as being recognized for their efforts.

There are people all around you every day who contribute in some way to your life and your work. Maybe you didn't notice them yesterday. Notice someone today, and you will make their day! ෬

෬

In every person who comes near you look for what is good and strong.

— JOHN RUSKIN

CHAPTER 10

൞

Thank Everybody for Everything!

*To live a life of gratitude is to
open our eyes to the countless ways
in which we are supported
by the world around us.
Such a life provides less space
for our suffering because
our attention is more balanced.
We are more often occupied
with noticing what we are given,
thanking those who have helped us,
and repaying the world in
some concrete way
for what we are receiving.*

— GREGG KRECH

When you think about the power you now realize you have, isn't it amazing?! It's not just Superman or Superwoman who has the power over good and evil. You have it, too. You have the power to control how you feel and what your outlook will be. What will you choose? We hope you'll choose a positive outlook!

You have the power to help others find happiness as well. All you have to do is say "thank you" and mean it. Dale Carnegie told us in *How to Win Friends and Influence People* that "Professor John Dewey, America's most profound philosopher… says the deepest urge in human nature is 'the desire to be important.'" Keep that in mind during the next conversation you have with someone. We know others like to talk about themselves. Why do you think that is? Could it be because they need to feel important? So why not help them? You listen and you make them feel important. At the very least, you may learn something insightful or helpful—what a concept! Then, when the conversation ends, genuinely thank that person for telling you so much about him or herself. It is probable that you just made a very good friend!

While Debbie and Craig were cruising on their sailboat, they met so many wonderful people. The cruising community is extremely close-knit. Nearly 100% of the cruisers they met were more than willing to come to the aid of a fellow boater, even if that fellow boater was a stranger, and usually without even being asked. When boaters see a need, they just jump right in. Even during a first time encounter with a fellow cruiser, it would not be unusual to be invited to dinner, where stories are shared and life-long relationships are built. Hard to imagine, but it's true.

Debbie remembers one particular evening when they had three new friends—a couple and a single man—from two different boats over for dinner. There was much discussion as everyone learned about each other. When the evening was nearly over, and everyone was getting tired, the single man, who was about 75 years old, told us he was a bronze sculptor. It gets better. He had been a laborer all his life with no training in metalwork. He had never been what he considered artistic and had never had an interest in art. When he retired 10 years prior, he tried sculpting as a hobby and found he had a remarkable talent. Today, his beautiful work is very much in demand.

Debbie found this gentleman and his story remarkable. She thinks of him often and, in fact, has told this story many times. She thanked him for telling his story because, not only did she learn something about sculpting, but he confirmed that everyone has a story or insight worth listening to, everyone is important and life can be just one extraordinary adventure after another! What wonderful lessons to learn from a man they had met only twice. So, help people feel important—listen to their stories and thank them for what they teach you. Appreciation is all about lifting others and that's what we should all be about. Let's thank everybody for everything!

Why wouldn't we help others feel important? Maybe we are afraid we won't have our time in the sun or we won't get our own story out. But when you find others important, aside from the benefits you will get from their stories and insights, they will find you important. Think about it. They like themselves, and surely you must like them, too, since you are listening to them. They will find you fascinating and they'll want to learn more about you! We think one of Dale Carnegie's most important lessons was that "You can make more friends in two months by becoming interested in other people than you can in two years by trying to get other people interested in you." We also think that, in addition to listening, expressing thanks to others is one of the best ways to help them feel important.

Abraham Lincoln wrote of the "craving" to be appreciated. Many others have echoed this sentiment over the years. We all know of our personal quest for appreciation. Here's what Dale Carnegie says about appreciation:

> There is a gnawing and unfaltering human hunger; and the rare individual who honestly satisfies this heart-hunger will hold people in the palm of his hand and "even the undertaker will be sorry when he dies."

Remember, genuine caring and appreciation will be returned to you ten-fold. Go have some fun and spread your joy by thanking everybody for everything! Thank you and God bless. ☙

☙

Try not to become a man of success but a man of value.

— ALBERT EINSTEIN

BE THANKFUL

Be thankful that you don't already have
everything you desire,
If you did, what would there be
to look forward to?

Be thankful when you don't
know something
For it gives you the opportunity to learn.

Be thankful for the difficult times.
During those times you grow.

Be thankful for your limitations
Because they give you opportunities
for improvement.

Be thankful for each new challenge
Because it will build your
strength and character.

Be thankful for your mistakes
They will teach you valuable lessons.

Be thankful when you're tired and weary
Because it means you've
made a difference.

It is easy to be thankful
for the good things.
A life of rich fulfillment comes
to those who are
also thankful for the setbacks.

GRATITUDE can turn a negative
into a positive.
Find a way to be thankful
for your troubles
and they can become your blessings.

— AUTHOR UNKNOWN

APPENDIX A

Gratitude Exercises (compiled)

EXERCISE ONE: Find time and a quiet place where you can reflect in private and uninterrupted peace. Reflect on your life—think of a time when you felt appreciation for something or someone. That time may be the present. That time may have been when you were in high school and had an inspiring teacher or coach. That time may have been the day your first child was born or when someone helped you in a time of need. Try to keep old or present negative emotions from blocking your memory. For this exercise, you are simply having a conversation with yourself. You don't have to share this conversation with anyone else, so be free with your thoughts and your feelings. Focus on remembering at least one instance of feeling genuine appreciation. When you find that moment, close your eyes, go back to the event and feel the emotion you felt then. Now, as that emotion consumes your heart and mind and brings you joy, you have the answer to the question—What are appreciation and gratitude?

EXERCISE TWO: Think about friends or family members who seem genuinely and consistently happy. Think especially of happy people who are not necessarily wealthy. Think of happy people who have suffered loss or serious illness. Do you find them to generally be people who exhibit positive or negative tendencies? Is their glass half full or half empty? Are their conversations centered around complaining or do they seem to be continually exploring and moving forward? Do they speak of blessings in their lives? Do they seem generally to enjoy and be grateful for people and circumstances? If you cannot find any happy people who are not wealthy and have not suffered loss, can you determine which came first... the wealth or the happiness... the wealth or the blessings? Seriously, were they born with a silver spoon? Have you never seen them cry? Go ahead and ask them if they feel blessed—and the role gratitude plays in their life. You might be surprised by the answer!

EXERCISE THREE: Identify at least one instance—more if you can—when someone in the past few days genuinely recognized you with appreciation or gratitude. Look back farther if you need to. Did anyone—a relative, a clerk in a store—say thank you to you today? Did someone recognize a project you completed—whether a report at work or a well-cooked meal at home? Did a neighbor tell you how nice your garden looks? Did someone wave to you while sitting in traffic when you allowed him or her in? Did you get an award or promotion recently? Did the postman, a neighbor or even a total stranger smile and wave at you for seemingly no reason at all? How does it feel to be recognized or appreciated?

EXERCISE FOUR: Since you are reading this book, you are likely in a place where you are comfortable and/or have some extra time. Take the time you have now to think about your life as it is at this moment. Think first about the people in your life—your family and friends in particular. Bring to mind as many family members and friends as you can and as you think of each one, think of at least one positive attribute of each person. Take your time doing this so you can really connect with your feelings for each person. Now think about your home. If you are home, get up and walk through each room. If you are somewhere else, make the walk in your mind. As you go into each room, make note of what you have. Think about how it feels to be home and what you like to do when you are home. Do you like to listen to music or play the piano? Do you like to play in the yard with your spouse or children? Cook? Entertain? Exercise? Read the newspaper while enjoying a cup of coffee or tea? Try to remember and even re-experience some of the activities you have enjoyed in your home. When you look around each room, look not only at the objects, but consider the memories associated with those objects and the activities you have enjoyed in that room. Again, try not to do this exercise quickly or abstractly. It can take time to unlock to the memories within.

When your mind is filled with warm thoughts of your loved ones and memories you care most about...

Now... imagine it's all gone... your family... your friends... your home... all that helps hold your memories... and all that would be a part of your future memories. Undoubtedly this is not a place you want to be! Now, remember that you do still have these precious people and these precious memories. Feel better? This is where the road to finding the gratitude within yourself can begin!

EXERCISE FIVE: From the moment you rise in the morning to the moment you close your eyes to sleep, there are innumerable opportunities for appreciation, even if it's just the flowers blooming in your neighbor's garden! The moment you open your eyes tomorrow, start looking for those opportunities. Don't get out of bed until you find at least one! You don't have to be creative or smart or educated or spiritual. You only have to open your eyes and your heart, and you only need take one moment... as many times a day as you can spare. Tomorrow do the same. The next day, and the next day, and the next day, do the same.

EXERCISE SIX: Today, thank someone for something, even if you think it is ordinary. In fact, thank everybody for everything! Thank your assistant for making the coffee in your office. Thank your spouse for emptying the dishwasher or taking out the trash or cleaning the toilet. Thank the bagger at your grocery store. Even if someone did something to aggravate you today, find something to thank him or her for. Did your son forget to take out the trash? Well, isn't there at least one thing you can thank him for today? Maybe he worked hard at school or work. Maybe he made his bed this morning or put his shoes away or walked the dog, even if you had to ask. Maybe he's sorry about the trash... now that's something to really be thankful for! Tomorrow thank someone else. Do the same thing each day following. There are a zillion things to thank people for!

EXERCISE SEVEN: Every day, identify at least three things you are grateful for and share your gratitude affirmations with someone you care about. Try to get your sharing partner to do the same—to share with you three things they are grateful for that day. Don't be too tough on your sharing partner at first. Just as it may have taken a while for you to get comfortable doing this, it may take him or her some time as well. If you feel like you don't have anyone to share this exercise with, you can do it alone—just write your three things down on a piece of paper or in a journal, and reflect on the abundance in your life.

EXERCISE EIGHT: Start a gratitude journal by writing every day about something or someone you are grateful for. Consider it a short note to yourself—just a sentence or two. You will not only feel good, but you are now creating a record of the joys in your life. When times are bad, we have to remember there were also good times. We have created a Gratitude Expressions journal that makes it easy to look back on past joys. In our five-year journal, each page represents five years of the same day, so every day when you write in your journal, the entry above is your entry on the same day from the prior year(s). It's fun and inspiring to look back on a positive moment from the same day on a prior year, and our journal makes that easy. So every day, you are writing about a present joy and you are looking back at past joys—happiness on top of happiness! Then, when something bad happens in your life—and we all have those times—looking back at the good times can help us realize that good times can and do exist!

EXERCISE NINE: Write a letter of gratitude. Think of someone who has contributed to your well-being or growth—someone you feel you have never really thanked. Most people will think of a parent or other adult mentor in their life, but it can be anyone... a teacher, a friend, a business colleague, a customer or the nurse who watched over a loved one in the hospital. Write a letter to that person describing the benefits that person bestowed upon you. Don't type it. Don't email it. Write it in your own handwriting. Be detailed in your description of their actions and how their actions made you feel. Then deliver the letter in person. Read it aloud to that person and take enough time to be together to share your feelings. P.S. Do not—we repeat, do not—do this without a box of tissues!

EXERCISE TEN: List everything you do to show appreciation to your current or potential clients or customers and referral sources. What else can you do? How often do they hear from you? How often do they hear from you without you trying to sell them something? How often do they hear simply that you are thinking of them? How many would recognize your name and welcome your call if you picked up the phone and called? How many would expect that you were just calling to talk business, sell or collect a fee? How many of your current or potential clients or customers and referral sources have you called this week simply to say hello?

EXERCISE ELEVEN: Today thank a client/customer/referral source for their business. Do the same tomorrow and every day following.

EXERCISE TWELVE: Today thank someone at work for something you feel is simply part of their job. Do the same thing tomorrow and every day following. Record your observations.

EXERCISE THIRTEEN: In your business, begin each regular team, sales and other meeting with a positive round—what's going well. End each meeting with recognition and appreciation. You can do a round robin so everyone gets a turn.

APPENDIX B

Resources and Recommended Reading

Deborah Norville. *Thank You Power, Making the Science of Gratitude Work for You.* Nashville: Robert Nelson, 2007.

Robert A. Emmons, Ph.D. *Thanks!* Boston: Houghton Mifflin Company, 2007.

Doc Lew Childre and Howard Martin, *The HeartMath Solution.* New York: Harper Collins, 2000.

Jordan Adler, *Beach Money.* Princeton: Accelerator Books, 2008.

Melody Beattie, *Gratitude: Affirming the Good Things in Life.* New York: Hazelden/Ballentine Books, 1992.

Dale Carnegie, *How to Win Friends and Influence People.* New York: Simon and Schuster, 1964.

Norman Vincent Peale, *The Power of Positive Thinking.* New York: Prentice-Hall, Inc., 1952.

Tommy Wyatt and Curtis Lewsey, *Appreciation Marketing.* Westport: BFC Group Publishing, 2009.

Mike Dooley, *Infinite Possibilities*, New York: Atria Books, 2009.

Ken Blanchard and Don Hutson, *The One Minute Entrepreneur*, Mechanicsburg: Executive Books, 2007.

Dr. Wayne Dyer, *Being in Balance- 9 Principles for Creating Habits to Match Your Desires*, Hay House, Inc., 2006.

Dr. Wayne Dyer, *The Power of Intention – Learning to Co-create Your World Your Way*, Hay House, Inc. 2004.

Esther and Jerry Hicks, *Money and the Law of Attraction – Learning to Attract Wealth, Health and Happiness*, Hay House Inc., 2008.

Esther and Jerry Hicks, *The Law of Attraction – The Basics of the Teaching of Abraham*, Hay House, Inc., 2006.

Marci Shimoff, *Happy for No Reason*, New York: Free Press, 2008.

Joe Vitale, *The Attractor Factor*, Hoboken: John Wiley & Sons, Inc., 2008.

Kody Bateman, *Promptings – Your Inner Guide to Making a Difference,* Salt Lake City: Eagle One Publishing, 2009.

ABOUT THE AUTHORS

DEBBIE ROSER, J.D.

Debbie Roser is an attorney, sailor, and entrepreneur committed to helping others see the blessings in their lives. From 2007 to 2009, Debbie underwent a life-altering and significant growth experience when she and her husband, Craig, left behind their home and work in Connecticut to cruise on their Island Packet sailboat, *Charmed*. They spent their time in the waters and ports off the East Coast of the United States, Bermuda and the Bahamas. Debbie discovered the cruising world is an amazing community of caring, loving and giving individuals—where everyone is accepted—and she and Craig made friendships that will last a lifetime. While cruising, Debbie partnered with friends, Radeen Cochran and Vanessa Williams, to launch an interactive website for women sailors to join together to learn from, and help each other.

Prior to her cruising hiatus, Debbie was a partner with Litchfield Cavo LLP, a national law firm, and practiced civil litigation in the Connecticut office. Now settling with her husband, Craig, in Sarasota, Florida, Debbie is happily closer to family and pursuing her dream of having her own business. As she evaluated the various business opportunities available, Debbie was most interested in one that would allow her to establish and maintain meaningful and positive relationships with others and her community. She found several opportunities that met these criteria.

Now, as an Independent Distributor with SendOutCards, Debbie teaches individuals and companies how to reach out to others with recognition and gratitude in a personal and heartfelt way. As a Senior Beauty Consultant with Mary Kay, Debbie helps women reach their potential for confidence and success. As Executive Director of the Sarasota Chapter of WOAMTEC, a networking organization designed to appeal to women in business, Debbie is committed to providing a forum where women can support each other in life and in business.

Debbie and Craig currently spend their free time exploring their new neighborhood, meeting their new neighbors and generally enjoying everything their new home town has to offer.

To learn more or to contact Debbie:
Debbie.Roser@gmail.com
DebbieRoser.WordPress.com
WmWAVES.com

PEGGY R. HOYT, J.D., M.B.A.

Peggy is an attorney, author and entrepreneur who reflects her passion for pets in almost everything she does. She comes by her love of animals naturally, as her father was the President and CEO of The Humane Society of the United States from 1970-1997.

Peggy and her law partner, Randy Bryan, own and operate Hoyt & Bryan, LLC—Family Wealth & Legacy Counsellors, in Oviedo, Florida. Both Peggy and Randy are Florida Bar board certified in Wills, Trusts and Estates. Their firm limits its practice to estate planning and elder law issues including the creation, maintenance and administration of estate plans that "work." Areas of expertise also include planning for special needs family members, unmarried couples, business succession and of course, pets.

This is Peggy's seventh book. Her first, *All My Children Wear Fur Coats How to Leave a Legacy for Your Pet*, (www.LegacyForYourPet.com) was inspired by her pets, currently three horses, four dogs and five cats. Subsequent co-authored books include *Special People, Special Planning-Creating a Safe Legal Haven for Families with Special Needs, Loving Without a License – An Estate Planning Survival Guide for Unmarried Couples and Same Sex Partners, A Matter of Trust – The Importance of Personal Instructions, Women in Transition –Navigating the Legal and Financial Challenges in Your Life* and *Like a Library Burning – Saving and Sharing Stories of a Lifetime*

In February 2009, Peggy and her best friend and estate planning colleague Teresa Morgan became SendOutCards Distributors calling themselves the Card Divas. They are currently Senior

Managers and use the SendOutCards system both personally and professionally in their daily lives by adopting the philosophy of "making a living through giving."

Peggy is active in a variety of organizations, including the National Network of Estate Planning Attorneys, Wealth Counsel and currently serves as Chair of the General Practice, Solo and Small Firm Section of the Florida Bar. She is a regular speaker on estate planning and elder law topics, as well as practice management including team training and marketing.

Peggy is married to Joe Allen and spends her "free" time training for limited distance endurance and competitive trail riding events on her Premarin rescue Sierra.

To learn more or to contact Peggy:
PeggyRHoyt@gmail.com
HoytBryan.com
PeggyRHoyt.blogspot.com

Gratitude Expressions

A FIVE-YEAR GRATITUDE JOURNAL

As a companion to *Thank Everybody for Everything! Grow Your Life and Business with Gratitude,* the authors have created a unique journal for recording, tracking and re-visiting your daily gratitude expressions over a five-year period. Each page of the journal is dedicated to one day and contains room for five entries—one for each of the five years represented by the journal. Every day when you write your gratitude expressions, you can look back and relive the blessings you experienced on the same day in the years prior. Each page also contains an inspirational quote as a gentle reminder of the value of gratitude and appreciation.

Once your written expressions become a habit, *Gratitude Expressions* will serve as a constant inspiration and provide you with a lifetime of treasured memories.

Gratitude Expressions is available wherever *Thank Everybody for Everything! Grow Your Life and Business with Gratitude* is sold, or you may contact the authors directly or visit *GratitudeExpressions.com*.

Praise for
Thank Everybody for Everything!

☙

"Thank Everybody for Everything! is a must read for any person who wants to enjoy life more. My goal in life is to be happy and to enjoy each day more and more. The only way I know how to do that is to appreciate everything and be grateful for what I have, and this book will show you how to do that. Anyone wishing to attract the best into their life will put this book at the top of their list."
—Adam Packard, Senior Executive, SendOutCards

"No one can read Thank Everybody for Everything! without feeling the incredible power of gratitude to enrich our lives. The 13 exercises will not only brighten the lives of others around you but will leave you feeling more positive and joyful. Thanks Peggy and Debbie for lighting the way for us!"
—John A. Warnick, creator of the
SEVEN SECRETS OF THE PURPOSEFUL TRUST

"If you want to achieve greater success—in your personal and professional life—without losing appreciation for the blessings already granted, you will find this book exceedingly useful. It draws from the experiences of both authors and offers simple techniques to help you live in gratitude."
—Kathleen Hawkins, President and Founder, WOAMTEC

"The number one human need after food, water and shelter is the need to feel appreciated. There is not a topic more important. Whether you are a business executive, entrepreneur or simply someone who wants to make a positive difference in the lives of others, you will benefit from Peggy and Debbie's book. I love it and I think you will too!"
—Jordan Adler, Entrepreneur and Author of BEACH MONEY–
CREATING YOUR DREAM LIFE THROUGH NETWORK MARKETING

"What a wonderful, thought provoking book. It blew me away! I particularly liked the exercises—they made me take action and show appreciation and gratitude to the people and things around me."
—Jim Packard, Senior Executive, SendOutCards

"Thank everybody for everything! What a concept! If you make it a sincere habit to express appreciation and gratitude, you will do better in every aspect of your life. Don't just say it. Mean it."
—Tommy Wyatt, co-author of the
national best-seller, APPRECIATION MARKETING:
HOW TO ACHIEVE GREATNESS THROUGH GRATITUDE